everyday novelli

More than 100 recipes from the nation's favourite French chef

Everyday Novelli

Jean-Christophe Novelli

headline

Dedicated from my heart to my parents, and with respect to Alexis Soyer (1810–1858), a very special Frenchman – born in France, buried in the UK – and also to my beautiful Michelle, the woman I love so, so much, forever.

First published in 2007 by
HEADLINE PUBLISHING GROUP

3

Cataloguing in Publication Data is available from the British Library

ISBN 978 0 7553 1717 2

Photography by Noel Murphy
Art direction by Smith & Gilmour, London
Designed by Smith & Gilmour, London
Typeset in PMN Caecilia by Smith & Gilmour, London
Colour reproduction, printing and binding by Rotolito Lombarda S.p.A. in Italy

Headline's policy is to use papers that are natural, renewable and recyclable products and made from wood grown in sustainable forests. The logging and manufacturing processes are expected to conform to the environmental regulations of the country of origin.

HEADLINE PUBLISHING GROUP
An Hachette Livre UK Company
338 Euston Road
London NW1 3BH

www.headline.co.uk
www.hodderheadline.com

Contents

'Jean brings glamour to the restaurant world. His capacity to give is extraordinary and what he has done for the industry should never be forgotten. Twenty years on, he is still like a brother to me'
Marco Pierre White

'I met Jean over fifteen years ago and he immediately struck me as a very creative young man. We went on and worked together in South Africa and I got to know him better and discovered what a likeable and brilliant craftsman he is. I am proud to say that he is a very special friend'
Raymond Blanc

'I have known Jean-Christophe since the late eighties and, with all my travels around the world, he is one of the most interesting cooks I have ever met and worked with, and definitely the best chef on TV today. I love him not only as a great friend but also like a son' Keith Floyd

'Jean-Christophe Novelli is one of the most singular chefs and also self taught; he is definitely one of the finest in Britain – if not the world. He creates rather than follows fashion' Jonathan Meads

For most of my life, family mealtimes have been very special – not just because everyone always enjoyed my humble cooking, but it was the only time I could get all of us sitting together around the same table. It was a time of love and passion, sometimes arguments, laughs, jokes and sharing stories on any subject; but, above all, it was about family interaction and I knew how fortunate we were to have those moments. I would like to say thank you to God and cooking!

When Jean-Christophe was a tiny nipper, every time I cooked, he would always be there, sticking his fingers into every bowl and pot. He was forever trying to get involved when I was busy in the kitchen. Because he was a very hyperactive and sometimes eccentric child from the day he was born, I assumed this behaviour was because he was hungry and impulsive, but I soon realised it wasn't the reason. In fact, as he became more expressive with me I made an unexpected discovery; despite him being a difficult child and being rejected from every school in the area, he felt the need to share his passion, expression, vision and, later, creativity. He became more and more attached to my daily cooking, and he was the only person who really understood that I used my cooking as a form of expression, so it would change according to my mood; and, through this, I was luckily able to inspire him. Our weekly visits to the market in Arras would electrify him with excitement and ideas – he loved the hustle and bustle, the colour, the aromas, the many varieties of food and local produce – and I loved to see my son so curious, passionate and illuminated by a subject, and to see him so eager to explore it at such an early age.

The first change started when he became a young baker. I can still hear him now taking his bike in the middle of the night to make his way to the bakery. Not only did he rapidly develop the potential of his five senses but he gained a massive amount of confidence and strength in his ability. By the age of fifteen he not only sounded like a man but there were already indications of the success which was to come, despite the fact that he still struggled to read and spell. I shall never forget the sad day he left France in the early eighties to fulfil his ambitions, grabbing the chance to discover Great Britain. Before walking out of our front door, he gave me a big hug and I remember him saying, 'Mother, I am now finally ready to leave and I am so grateful to have learnt so much from you and my grandmothers [Louise and Germaine], which will allow me to move on and discover more about life and express myself.'

His celebrity status hasn't changed him, nor have his numerous culinary recognitions and awards – even receiving the merit of an Honorary Degree of Doctor of Arts. I'm glad to say he is still that same kind, humble boy.

I am so proud of my son and especially his book *Everyday Novelli*, not because I am a part of it but simply because I believe it is full of honest, accessible and versatile recipes. They may ask for a little effort but you will get exciting results – all with my son's special twist. They are for everybody to enjoy good cooking and, most importantly, to have fun. Finding happiness is what life is all about. You must use them to express yourself and, above all, share them with the people you love.

BREAKFAST AND BRUNCH

Wake-up Smoothie
Waffles
Spiced Mixed Berries with Yogurt
My Garden Jam
Flemish Tart
Baked Spiced Clementines
Poached Salmon, Leek and Blue
  Cheese Quiche
Brioche
Croque Madame
Spiced Aubergine Wrapped in Parma Ham
Royal Egg Flan Trio
Crouchmoor Farm Breakfast

Wake-up Smoothie

So easy to make, this smoothie is a great way to start the day. If you want to get the best out of your smoothie and you don't want to lose any of the vitamins, drink it as soon as you make it and don't over blitz. Or you can leave it to chill overnight.

SERVES: 2
PREPARATION TIME: 10 MINUTES

200g Braeburn apples, cored and chopped
 but left unpeeled
397ml condensed milk
200g fresh or frozen raspberries
½ banana
1 kiwi, peeled and chopped

100g pomegranate seeds
juice of ½ lemon
175ml Greek yogurt
To decorate
4–6 fresh mint leaves, shredded

1. In a blender or food processor, blitz the apple, condensed milk, raspberries, banana, kiwi and pomegranate seeds until blended.

2. Pass the mixture through a sieve.

3. Stir in the lemon juice and fold in the Greek yogurt.

4. Serve in tall glasses, decorated with the mint.

Pomegranate seeds are available prepacked from supermarkets. For a sweeter taste, add a little runny honey. For a bit of variety, change one of the ingredients each time you make it.

Waffles

Sometimes at the end of the month, when times were difficult, my mother would make this waffle recipe for tea – light, fluffy and homemade, they are ideal for getting children involved. Serve them warm with fresh fruit and coconut cream. You will need a waffle iron for this recipe.

SERVES: 4
PREPARATION TIME: 10 MINUTES
COOKING TIME: 12 MINUTES

60g plain flour
30g cornflour
1/2 teaspoon salt
1/2 teaspoon baking powder
1/4 teaspoon bicarbonate of soda
180ml buttermilk

50ml milk
6 tablespoons vegetable oil
1 large egg, separated
1 tablespoon caster sugar
a few drops vanilla extract

1. Preheat the oven to 200°C/Fan 180°C/Gas 6. Preheat the waffle iron. Sift the flours together into a medium bowl and add the salt, baking powder and bicarb.

2. Mix the buttermilk, milk and vegetable oil in a jug; beat in the egg yolk and set aside.

3. In another bowl, beat the egg white to the soft peak stage. Sprinkle in the sugar and continue to beat until the egg white is stiff and glossy. Beat in the vanilla extract.

4. Pour the buttermilk into the dry ingredients and whisk until just incorporated. Drop the whipped egg white on to the batter in dollops and fold each in gently with a spatula until just incorporated before adding the next.

5. Pour a thin layer of the batter on to the hot waffle iron and cook until the waffle is crisp and golden brown: this should take roughly 3–5 minutes. Set the cooked waffle directly on the shelf in the preheated oven to keep it warm and crisp. Repeat with the remaining batter, keeping the cooked waffles warm in the oven.

6. When all the waffles are cooked, serve immediately with fresh raspberries and coconut cream (see page 237).

As a natural alternative, you can substitute the sugar with clear honey.

Spiced Mixed Berries with Yogurt

I make this a lot when the soft summer fruits are in season. I am lucky enough to be able to pick them from my own garden. The spices bring this dish to life and if you leave it to mellow overnight the flavours are even more enhanced. It is a fantastic medley of fruits and yogurt blended together.

SERVES: 3–4
PREPARATION TIME: 5–6 MINUTES
COOKING TIME: 10 MINUTES
CHILLING TIME: 4–6 HOURS

1 star anise
1 cinnamon stick
100g raspberries
100g strawberries, hulled and sliced in half
100g redcurrants
100g blackcurrants
100g blueberries

1 vanilla pod, halved lengthways
50g acacia honey
20ml water
lemon juice
To serve
Greek yogurt
sprigs fresh mint

1. Preheat a large, heavy-based pan until very hot. In the dry pan, pan-fry the star anise and cinnamon for 2–3 minutes to release the aromas, then add the fruits and vanilla, and cook, shaking the pan, for another 3 minutes.

2. Add the honey and allow to melt, undisturbed, for 2 minutes or until the fruit is coated in the syrup.

3. Add the water and a splash of lemon juice to taste. Allow to cook, undisturbed, for 1 more minute to infuse.

4. Remove from the heat, turn into a glass or ceramic dish, and leave overnight in the fridge to chill.

5. Remove the vanilla pod. Serve chilled with a dollop of yogurt and a sprig of mint.

If the above fruits are not in season, use frozen fruits, thawed, which will have just as much vitamin C as fresh.

My Garden Jam

This is an anytime jam that can be made from fresh or frozen raspberries. Serve with homemade scones or use it as a filling for cakes, like Victoria sandwich, and tarts. You will need a cook's thermometer for this recipe.

MAKES: 700–800G
PREPARATION TIME: 5–10 MINUTES
COOKING TIME: 40–50 MINUTES

310g caster sugar
1kg ripe raspberries
110g caster sugar, mixed with 30g dried pectin
juice of 1 lemon

1. Place the sugar in a heavy-based pan and warm over a medium heat until it has melted, stirring constantly with a wooden spoon. Add the raspberries and stir to combine, breaking them up a little.

2. Cover with a lid and boil rapidly for 5 minutes. Remove the lid and cook for a further 5 minutes or until the temperature reaches 100°C.

3. Skim off any impurities, then sprinkle in the combined sugar and pectin, together with the lemon juice. Stir well and cook for another 2–3 minutes.

4. Meanwhile, put the sealed jars in a large pan of cold water, bring slowly to the boil and simmer for 20–25 minutes, timing this from when the water reaches boiling point. Remove the jars with tongs and leave to cool.

5. Check whether the jam has reached its setting point by placing a small amount on a cold saucer and putting it in the fridge for 2–3 minutes. If it has reached setting point, the jam should wrinkle when pushed with a finger.

6. Pour the jam into the clean sterilised jars, using a funnel, and seal with a screw top, then leave to cool. Label and store in a cool dark place. The jam will keep for up to 1 year. Once opened, the jam should be stored in the fridge.

Preserving sugar, which has the pectin already added, is available from supermarkets.

This recipe works equally well with strawberries, blackberries, or a mixture of fruits or berries. Simply adjust the amount of sugar depending on the sweetness of the fruit.

Flemish Tart

This is a great recipe despite the fact that I hate onions. I remember well how I used to have to cut up what seemed like millions of onions when I worked at the bakery in Arras. Leave the fat on the bacon as it adds to the flavour of the finished tart. This is my mother's recipe with a twist.

SERVES: 4
PREPARATION TIME: 20 MINUTES
FREEZER TIME: 10 MINUTES
COOKING TIME: 30 MINUTES

vegetable oil
25g butter
1 very large onion, peeled and finely chopped
1 large leek, cleaned and finely chopped
150g smoked back bacon, cut into chunks

225ml crème fraîche (or fromage frais)
salt and freshly ground black pepper
4 pinches freshly grated nutmeg
1 bay leaf
1 x 150g packet ready-made shortcrust pastry

1. Preheat the oven to 220°C/Fan 200°C/Gas 7. Oil a 35 x 23cm baking sheet.

2. Heat the butter in a frying pan and over a very low heat cook the onion and leek, stirring constantly, for about 8–10 minutes, until soft, golden and melting.

3. At the same time, in another frying pan, dry-fry the bacon until it is lightly browned.

4. In a bowl, combine the crème fraîche, seasoning, nutmeg and bay leaf.

5. On a lightly floured surface, roll out the shortcrust pastry until it is slightly larger than the baking sheet and lay it on the sheet. Make a raised edge, by pinching your thumb and forefinger together all around the edge of the pastry. Put the baking sheet into the freezer for about 10 minutes or until the pastry is firm.

6. Remove the baking sheet from the freezer and bake the pastry in the preheated oven for 10–12 minutes.

7. Remove from the oven and cover the pastry with the onions and leeks, scattering the bacon evenly over them. Pour over the crème fraîche, removing and discarding the bay leaf. Return the pastry to the preheated oven and bake for 15 minutes or until the top is lightly glazed. Serve hot.

If wished, add a little beer, cider or stout – 100ml at most – to the onions while they are gently cooking. This reduces down while the onions are softening, adding enormous flavour.

Baked Spiced Clementines

This dish always reminds me of Christmas and, indeed, it is best made with slightly overripe clementines, the ones no one ever eats in the overflowing fruit bowl at Christmas. It makes a great breakfast dish (omitting the alcohol), but you can also serve it as a dessert with ice-cream. Remember that you can eat the skins, too, as they have been blanched and dewaxed.

SERVES: 4
PREPARATION TIME: 15 MINUTES
COOKING TIME: 20–25 MINUTES, PLUS 12 HOURS DRYING TIME, OR OVERNIGHT

4 large clementines or oranges
2 vanilla pods, split into 4 pieces
4 star anise
80g icing sugar

To finish
about 40ml kirsch, whisky or Cointreau (optional)
icing sugar
crème fraîche or vanilla ice-cream

1. Preheat the oven to its maximum.

2. Blanch the clementines in boiling water for 1 minute. Remove with a slotted spoon and drain. Pierce the top of each and insert 1 piece of vanilla pod and 1 star anise. Dust with the icing sugar.

3. When the oven has been at its maximum for 10 minutes, switch it off. Gently place the clementines on a wire rack in a baking tray and put into the oven, which will still be very hot. Leave to bake or 'confit' overnight, or for at least 12 hours.

4. When the clementines are 'confited' they can be kept in the fridge until you need them. When you are ready to serve, preheat the oven to 180°C/Fan 160°C/Gas 4. If you are serving the clementines at dinner for a dessert, make a hole in the top and spoon a little kirsch into each one.

5. Sprinkle with icing sugar and bake in the preheated oven for 2–3 minutes. Remove and sprinkle again with icing sugar. Return to the hot oven to glaze for 2–3 minutes more.

6. Just prior to serving, cut the clementines in half, and top each with a dollop of crème fraîche or ice-cream, mixed with a little kirsch if wished.

If clementines are not in season, choose another type of easy peeler like mandarins or satsumas. Instead of vanilla and star anise, you can also use cinnamon, rosemary, liquorice or lavender.

Poached Salmon, Leek and Blue Cheese Quiche

Salmon and Stilton make a great combination, and I make this quiche with leeks because, to be honest, I don't really like onions. This cream and egg mix can form the basis of any flan or quiche. The flaked almonds added at the last minute give a lovely crunch. If possible, make sure your salmon comes from Scotland. This is an ideal brunch dish.

SERVES: 6–8
PREPARATION TIME: 35 MINUTES
COOKING TIME: 30 MINUTES

1 x 150g packet ready-made shortcrust pastry, plus 1 egg, beaten, or 1 x 20cm ready-made pastry case

Poached salmon
600ml water
1 carrot, peeled and sliced
1 onion, peeled and sliced
1 celery stalk, sliced
2 star anise, or ½ fennel bulb
2–3 black peppercorns
1 bay leaf
1 teaspoon salt
1 tablespoon white wine vinegar
1 x 500g piece of wild or farmed salmon on the bone

Filling
50g butter
2 large leeks, cleaned and sliced
salt and freshly ground black pepper
1 teaspoon Pernod or Ricard
10 fresh basil leaves, torn in big pieces
10 fresh tarragon leaves, torn in big pieces
150–200g blue cheese, preferably Stilton, crumbled
2 large eggs
275ml double cream
pinch freshly grated nutmeg
handful flaked almonds

1. Preheat the oven to 180°C/Fan 160°C/Gas 4.

2. First make the court-bouillon, which is useful for poaching fish in general. Put all the ingredients, with the exception of the salmon, into a large saucepan. Bring to the boil and simmer for 20 minutes.

3. Remove from the heat, and slip the salmon into the pan, cover and leave undisturbed for about 5 minutes. The fish should still be pink in the middle. It is important not to overcook it. Drain the fish from the liquid.

4. When it is cool enough to handle, skin the fish, and remove all the bones. Flake the flesh into quite large pieces.

5. If using ready-made pastry, roll it out and use to line a 20cm flan ring, laid on a baking sheet. Prick the base, line with greaseproof paper, and fill with baking beans. Bake blind in the preheated oven for about 20 minutes or until the pastry is set.

6. Remove from the oven and carefully take out the greaseproof paper and baking beans. Put to one side.

7. To make the filling, melt the butter in a pan and gently cook the leeks until soft, roughly 2–3 minutes. Season, turn into a bowl and add the Pernod or Ricard, herbs and cheese. Cover with cling film, and leave to macerate for about 5 minutes.

8. Arrange the leek filling and the salmon flakes on the base of the quiche case.

9. Beat together the eggs and double cream, and season. Pour into the quiche case, then sprinkle the top with the nutmeg and flaked almonds.

10. Bake in the preheated oven – at the same temperature as before – for 20–30 minutes or until set.

11. Remove from the oven and allow to cool slightly before serving, perhaps with some rocket leaves dressed with a little olive oil and lemon juice, and some cherry tomatoes.

Smoked haddock and prawns can be substituted for the salmon.

Brioche

The smell of homemade brioche is wonderful and the taste is even better. Serve it in slices for breakfast or tea and, if you have any left over the next day, use it to make the best ever bread and butter pudding. The brioche will freeze well.

SERVES: 8–10
PREPARATION TIME: 1 HOUR
COOKING TIME: 25 MINUTES

1kg plain flour, sifted
140g caster sugar
20g salt
60g fresh yeast
250g unsalted butter

5 medium eggs
300ml full-fat milk
¼ vanilla pod
1 medium egg yolk
1 teaspoon olive oil

1. In a large bowl, mix together the flour, sugar, salt, yeast and butter. Add the eggs one at a time, combining each thoroughly before adding the next.

2. Meanwhile, heat the milk gently in a saucepan, add the vanilla and allow to infuse. Do not allow the milk to boil. After about 3 minutes, remove the vanilla pod and gradually add the milk to the dough, beating well until it is all absorbed.

3. Once the dough detaches from the sides of the bowl, it is ready to place into a loaf tin to prove. Once the brioche has risen, knock it back down, as it will then rise a lot more.

4. Towards the end of the proving time, preheat the oven to 200°C/Fan 180°C/Gas 5.

5. When the dough is ready to be put in the oven, mix the egg yolk and the olive oil and brush the top of the loaf, this will help achieve a beautiful golden, glazed finish.

6. Bake the brioche in the preheated oven for 10 minutes, reduce the temperature to 160°C/Fan 180°C/Gas 3 and leave it for a further 15 minutes, until it is golden brown and comes out of the mould easily.

7. Leave it to cool and then serve.

If you use baking parchment in the mould, you will need to remove the brioche near the end of the cooking time and return it (without the mould) to the oven for 5 minutes to finish. This prevents the base from being moist.

As a variation, you could sprinkle the dough with almonds before baking.

Croque Madame

When I worked in a café as a boy, croque monsieur was on the menu, but it never sold very well. (I know, because I was the one who was supposed to make them!) One day a new waiter arrived and he suggested changing the name of the dish to 'madame', serving it for breakfast and putting an egg on the top. It became the most popular snack of the café.

SERVES: 4
PREPARATION TIME: 5–6 MINUTES
COOKING TIME: 10 MINUTES

8 slices white bread
70g unsalted butter, softened
225g Gruyère cheese, cut into thin slices
340g smoked ham, such as Black Forest,
   cut into 12–16 thin slices

fleur de sel or salt and freshly ground black
   pepper, to taste
4 extra-large eggs

1. To assemble the croque madames, set the slices of bread on a board and butter one side of them.

2. Turn over half of them, so that they are buttered side down, and cover with the cheese slices, folding the cheese back towards the middle if it extends over the edges of the bread.

3. Lay 3–4 slices of ham in an even layer over the cheese, then cover with the top slice of bread, buttered side up.

4. Gently pan-fry the croque madames in half of the remaining softened butter, turning once, until nicely golden brown.

5. While they are cooking, heat the last of the butter in another pan and fry the eggs.

6. Serve each croque madame piping hot, topped with a fried egg.

Low-fat mayonnaise mixed with a little mustard can be added as well – spread on the cheese-side of the bread.

Spiced Aubergine Wrapped in Parma Ham

When buying aubergines make sure they are firm to touch and free from bruising, and that they have a fresh-looking green stalk. This is a stunning dish and the flavours of Parma ham and cheese blend so well together. When making the roux, using warmed milk will help incorporate it.

SERVES: 4
PREPARATION TIME: 10 MINUTES
COOKING TIME: 20–25 MINUTES

1 large aubergine, trimmed and quartered
juice of 1 lemon
3 sprigs fresh thyme, stalks removed
2 bay leaves
1 small garlic clove, peeled and finely
  chopped
40ml extra-virgin olive oil
generous pinch caster sugar
100ml stout
4 pancakes (see page 216)

8 slices Parma ham
100g Cheddar cheese, cut into 4 thin slices
Roux
25g butter
25g plain flour
150ml milk, warmed
1 teaspoon freshly grated nutmeg
75g Gruyère or Emmenthal cheese, grated
salt and freshly ground black pepper
generous pinch paprika

1. Preheat the oven to 180°C/Fan 160°C/Gas 4.

2. Lay the aubergine quarters in a non-metallic dish. Sprinkle with the lemon juice, the herbs and the garlic, and leave to sweat for 2–3 minutes.

3. Heat the oil in an ovenproof casserole. Turn the aubergine into it, removing the bay leaves. Add the sugar and the stout.

4. Bake in the preheated oven until the aubergine is soft and the liquor is syrupy, roughly 10–12 minutes. Remove the aubergine, drain and leave to cool. Reserve the liquor, measuring out 50ml.

5. To make the roux, melt the butter in a small saucepan. Add the flour and cook, stirring constantly, for 1–2 minutes or until the flour is cooked – but do not allow it to brown. Pour in the warmed milk gradually, stirring constantly with a wooden spoon to prevent lumps forming, and when all the milk is incorporated bring to the boil.

6. Stir in the aubergine liquor and nutmeg to taste. Add the grated cheese and season to taste. Stir thoroughly to combine.

7. Wrap a cooked pancake and 2 slices of Parma ham around each section of cooled aubergine. Top each one with a slice of Cheddar and lay in an ovenproof gratin dish.

8. Pour over the roux and sprinkle with the paprika. Return to the hot oven for 10 minutes or until the roux is bubbling. Serve immediately.

Royal Egg Flan Trio

This may look complicated, and I suppose it is a little, but really you are just making three straightforward versions of the same basic mix. The egg and cream custard is divided in three, and a different colour – green spinach, white cheese and red tomato – is added to each. The cooking thereafter is simple and the result is spectacular. If you can find glass moulds, the coloured layers show up beautifully and you need not turn out the flans when serving.

SERVES: 6
PREPARATION TIME: 15 MINUTES
COOKING TIME: 1 HOUR 5 MINUTES

1 litre double cream
10 large eggs, beaten
2 teaspoons chopped garlic
salt and freshly ground black pepper
Tomato
100g tomato purée
Cheese
200g Emmenthal, Beaufort cheese
  or blue stilton, grated

Spinach
150g spinach, washed, cooked and
  squeezed dry of excess water
30g fresh basil leaves, finely chopped
To serve
1 quantity aromatic cream sauce
  (see page 217)

1. Preheat the oven to 140°C/Fan 120°C/Gas 1. Grease with butter six pudding moulds, about 8cm across and about 8cm high, or large ramekins.

2. Mix the cream with the eggs and garlic, and season. Divide equally between three bowls.

3. To prepare the flavourings, add the tomato purée to the first bowl. Add the cheese to the second. Chop the spinach very finely, add the basil, and turn into the third. Use a hand blender to combine each mix thoroughly.

4. Place the greased moulds in a bain-marie or roasting tray. Pour the red tomato mixture into all six moulds. Pour enough boiling water into the bain-marie or roasting tray to come halfway up the sides of the moulds, and bake in the preheated oven for about 25 minutes or until just set.

5. Remove the bain-marie or roasting tray from the oven, and pour the white cheese mixture into the moulds on top of the set tomato mixture. Return to the hot oven, and bake for 20 minutes, or until the cheese mixture is set.

6. Again remove the bain-marie or roasting tray from the oven, and pour the spinach mixture into the moulds on top of the set cheese mixture. This should fill the moulds to the top. Return the bain-marie or roasting tray to the hot oven and bake for 20 minutes or until the spinach mixture has set in its turn.

7. While the moulds are baking, make the aromatic cream sauce (see page 217).

8. Remove the bain-marie or roasting tray from the oven and carefully lift out the moulds.

9. When the butter sauce is ready, remove the flans from the moulds by carefully loosening around the edges with a knife and upturning them on to serving plates. Serve immediately with the hot sauce.

A splash of Pernod in the spinach enhances the flavour.

Crouchmoor Farm Breakfast

Once in a while at the farm – on a day when we can take our time – we indulge in what we call our Crouchmoor Farm Breakfast. It is a great favourite of mine. It makes a leisurely start, especially if there are no classes at the academy or other obligations. Ideal before a long country walk or while reading the Sunday papers. Buy the best possible ingredients and, after a breakfast like this, you are guaranteed to have a great day – and you won't be hungry again until at least mid-afternoon!

SERVES: 2
PREPARATION TIME: 5 MINUTES
COOKING TIME: 25 MINUTES

olive oil
2 small sausages (any variety)
1 sprig fresh rosemary
2 sprigs fresh thyme
3 large garlic cloves, peeled and halved
1 small black pudding (preferably a French boudin noir)
1 teaspoon cumin seeds
1 large beef tomato, cut in half horizontally

50g Cheddar cheese, sliced
pinch paprika
4 smoked bacon rashers
2 Portobello mushrooms, peeled but left whole
white wine vinegar
2 duck eggs
2 tablespoons hollandaise
2 sprigs fresh chervil

1. Have ready a couple of frying pans (one of which should be ovenproof), as well as a pan for boiling water. Preheat the grill to high, and the oven to 160°C/Fan 140°C/Gas 3.

2. Heat a heavy-based frying pan with 1 tablespoon of the oil, and add the sausages, rosemary, half the thyme and two of the garlic cloves. Fry for about 10 minutes.

3. Bring the pan of water to the boil and put in the black pudding for 2–3 minutes to soften the skin. Remove the pudding with a slotted spoon and add it whole to the pan with the sausages. Watch out as the water on the black pudding will make the oil spit. Cook the black pudding evenly on all sides, roughly 10 minutes.

4. Heat another frying pan, which should be ovenproof, and add a splash of olive oil and the cumin seeds. Toast them for 1 minute and then add the tomato halves, cut side down first, together with the remaining thyme and garlic. Fry for 2–3 minutes, then turn over and fry the other side for 2–3 more minutes, by which time the tomatoes should be soft and brown all over.

5. Lay the cheese slices with a pinch of paprika on top of the tomato halves and bake in the preheated oven or under the grill for about 5 minutes, or until the cheese is melted.

6. When the sausages are brown and they have been cooking for 10 minutes or so, remove with the black pudding to the preheated oven to keep warm. Clean the pan, add about 1 tablespoon olive oil, and add the bacon and the mushrooms. Fry until the bacon is crisp on both sides and the mushrooms have softened.

7. Meanwhile, bring the pan of water back to the boil and add a splash of vinegar. Crack each egg separately into a bowl, then transfer to a ladle and gently tip into the water. Leave the eggs to poach for around 2 minutes. Remove them with a slotted spoon, trim off the excess white with kitchen scissors and keep warm.

8. To assemble, have ready two warm plates and place one mushroom in the centre of each. Cover it with a tomato half. Arrange the sausage, black pudding and bacon to one side. Place a warm poached egg on the other side, topped with a spoonful of hollandaise, and garnished with a sprig of chervil. Serve immediately with brown toast.

If you put the cheese in the freezer for an hour before you need it, this makes slicing easier. If you don't have any hollandaise, mix 1 tablespoon mayonnaise with 1 teaspoon English mustard and a pinch of medium curry powder.

LUNCH

Sweet Gazpacho with Herby
  Crab Mayonnaise
French Country-style Pâté
Baby Squid, Chorizo, Black Pudding,
  Anchovy and Poached Egg Salad
Anchovy, Goat's Cheese and Orange Salad
Confit of Sole Andalou
Pork Mince Croquettes with Sweet
  Chilli Dip
Chou Farci
Tuna Steak Tartare Rapido
Minute-poached Salmon and
  Gorgonzola Rigatoni
Sweet Curried Seafood Stew with Beer
Strawberry and Lemongrass Skewers
Crème Légère Monique
Bitter Chocolate and Honeycomb Parfait
Exotic Fruit Ice Parfait
Tartes Fines with Pineapple and Chilli

Sweet Gazpacho with Herby Crab Mayonnaise

This is a great Spanish recipe that always reminds me of some good friends, Tino and Miranda from Rucola and Rocket, but I have treated it to a French touch. All it takes is simple preparation and a bit of help from a food processor or liquidiser. If your food processor is too small just blitz the ingredients in two batches.

SERVES: 4
PREPARATION TIME: 15–20 MINUTES
FREEZER/CHILLING TIME: 1 HOUR

Gazpacho
500g beef tomatoes, roughly chopped
20g fresh green chillies, deseeded
100ml extra virgin olive oil
2 teaspoons caster sugar
30–45ml white wine vinegar
1 garlic clove, peeled
⅓ cucumber
1 teaspoon English mustard
2 teaspoons fresh coriander, chopped
salt
Crab Mayonnaise
100g very fresh white crab meat, flaked

100ml mayonnaise
⅓ cucumber, deseeded (use the seeds in the gazpacho) and cut into small, even chunks
2 anchovy fillets (optional), drained and cut into small pieces
½ garlic clove, peeled and finely chopped
10g fresh chives, snipped into 2cm lengths
6 fresh basil leaves, chopped
juice of 1 lemon
1 teaspoon mild curry powder
salt and freshly ground black pepper

1. First, make the gazpacho – ensure all the ingredients are at room temperature. In a blender or food processor, blitz the tomatoes for 10–15 seconds. Add the remaining ingredients and blitz until smooth. If the mixture is still stiff, add a little water and blitz again until you have the desired consistency. Pour into a large jug, cover and chill in the fridge for at least 1 hour.

2. For the crab mayonnaise, in a large bowl combine the crab meat, mayonnaise, cucumber, anchovies (if using), garlic, chives, basil, lemon juice, curry powder and seasoning.

3. To serve, pour the chilled soup into serving bowls and put a dollop of the crab mayonnaise in the centre of each.

Use glass containers to chill the finished soup as glass is a good cold conductor.

French Country-style Pâté

A classic pâté like this is very common in France. Here I have tried to simplify it as much as possible, although you need to remember that you have to start it two days before you want to eat it. Adding an egg white would make it a little finer in texture. You could also wrap the cooked pâté in a bread dough (see page 170) and, after proving, bake at 180°C for 30–35 minutes. Serve the terrine from the dish, rather than turning it out. This not only helps it to retain its shape but also makes it keep better.

MAKES: 1 TERRINE, TO SERVE 12
PREPARATION TIME: 20 MINUTES
CHILLING TIME: 24 HOURS
COOKING TIME: 1$\frac{1}{2}$ HOURS
MARINATING TIME: 24 HOURS

80ml port
40ml brandy
15g caster sugar
30g sea salt
10g freshly ground black pepper
360g chicken livers, cleaned and chopped
430g pork back fat, minced
530g shoulder of pork, minced

100g flat-leaf parsley, finely chopped
6 garlic cloves, peeled and finely chopped
10g medium curry powder
10g fresh thyme, stalks removed
To finish
12–16 thin slices pancetta
4 bay leaves

1. Put the port, brandy, sugar and 10g of the salt and 3g of the pepper into a glass or ceramic dish, and add the chicken livers. Combine thoroughly, cover with cling film and leave to marinate in the fridge for 24 hours.

2. In a large bowl, mix together the minced pork fat and pork shoulder with the chicken livers and the marinade, then add the parsley, garlic, curry powder, thyme and the remaining salt and pepper. Combine thoroughly.

3. Preheat the oven to 170°C/Fan 160°C/Gas 3.

4. Line the base and sides of a lidded, heavy-based terrine dish with the slices of pancetta, leaving the ends overhanging the top of the dish. Turn the meat mixture into the dish, pack down and lay the bay leaves on top. Fold over the overhanging pancetta so that the terrine mix is completely covered. Either return the pâté to the fridge for 1 hour or so at this stage, to marinate further, or cook straightaway.

5. Put the lid on the terrine, and bake in the preheated oven for 1½ hours.

6. When cooked, remove from the oven and leave to cool in the terrine. When completely cold, keep in the fridge for at least 24 hours before slicing.

Baby Squid, Chorizo, Black Pudding, Anchovy and Poached Egg Salad

In the summer, I sometimes use this recipe for the course at my academy or for eating at home on the patio. It's perfect for lunch with a nice glass of medium and fruity white wine. When the chorizo is cooking, the delicious smell filters out to the garden and stimulates appetites!

SERVES: 4
PREPARATION TIME: 25 MINUTES
COOKING TIME: 15 MINUTES

100g chorizo sausage, sliced
10 baby squid, cleaned
1 garlic clove, peeled and crushed
juice of ½ lemon
250g smoked pancetta, cut into small lardons
500g black pudding (preferably a French boudin noir)

salt and freshly ground black pepper
1 tablespoon white wine vinegar
4 large eggs
1 frisée lettuce, prepared (see tip)
150ml anchovyade (see page 223)

1. Preheat the oven to 180°C/Fan 160°C/Gas 4.

2. Heat a heavy frying pan until very hot, then add the slices of chorizo. Fry gently until golden, then remove with a slotted spoon to a suitable container, leaving the chorizo oil in the pan. Set aside.

3. Add the squid to the chorizo oil in the pan, together with the garlic and lemon juice, and fry gently for 3–4 minutes. Remove with a slotted spoon and add to the chorizo.

4. In the same pan fry the pancetta lardons until nicely coloured. Remove with a slotted spoon and add to the squid and chorizo.

5. Bring a saucepan of water to the boil, and plunge in the black pudding. Blanch for 10 seconds, then remove with a slotted spoon and put into an ovenproof dish. Leave the water boiling. Season the black pudding, and bake in the preheated oven for 10 minutes. When cool enough to handle, cut into big chunks.

6. In the meantime, add the vinegar to the boiling water, crack the eggs then slide them in. Poach for 4 minutes, then remove, using a slotted spoon. Trim the whites if wished.

7. To assemble, cut the required amount of frisée (refrigerate the remainder) and put in a large bowl. Add the chorizo, squid, pancetta lardons, black pudding and three quarters of the anchovyade, and stir gently to combine.

8. Divide the salad between four plates, and top each portion with a poached egg. Add 1 teaspoon or so of water to the remaining mayonnaise to thin it and drizzle over the top of the eggs. Serve immediately.

A frisée lettuce needs careful attention before use. Wash it, then immerse, leafy head down, in a bowl of water. Refrigerate for 24 hours, which crisps it up wonderfully. Drain well, then put in a cloth or salad spinner to remove excess water. Keep in the fridge until required.

Anchovy, Goat's Cheese and Orange Salad

The combination of flavours makes this recipe a winner before you've even started. I use St Maure's goat's cheese but do use your favourite one – there's some great quality British goat's cheese on the market now.

SERVES: 4 AS A STARTER OR 2 AS A MAIN COURSE
PREPARATION TIME: 10 MINUTES
COOKING TIME: 20 MINUTES

3–4 large oranges
1 teaspoon caster sugar
¼ vanilla pod, halved lengthways
4 cardamom seeds
1 garlic clove, peeled
4 fresh basil leaves, torn
8 slices baguette

50ml olive oil
8 slices goat's cheese (e.g. St Maure)
100ml extra-virgin olive oil
4–6 anchovy fillets, chopped
1 tablespoon grainy mustard
1 head of frisée lettuce, prepared (see page 39)

1. Preheat the oven to 160°C/Fan 140°C/Gas 6.

2. First make the dressing. Squeeze the oranges and pour the juice into a saucepan with the sugar, vanilla pod and cardamom seeds.

3. On a very gentle heat, cook until the juice has been reduced to a syrup, roughly 15–20 minutes.

4. Remove from the heat, add the garlic and basil, and leave the dressing to infuse.

5. Lay the baguette slices on a baking sheet. Drizzle the olive oil over them and cover each slice with the cheese.

6. Bake in the preheated oven for 10 minutes, or until the cheese has melted.

7. In a bowl, combine the extra-virgin olive oil, anchovies and mustard, and add to the dressing.

8. Cut the frisée lettuce into pieces with scissors. Add to the dressing and stir gently to coat the leaves.

9. Divide the salad between the baguette slices and serve immediately.

Make sure the oranges are not too acidic. When reducing the orange juice, do so very slowly, ensuring that it does not boil.

Confit of Sole Andalou

This dish reminds me of Pierre Chevilliard, a great man who I met 25 years ago when I first arrived in Britain. Actually, Pierre's the only head chef I've ever had. He was working alongside one of the finest restaurant managers ever, Guiseppe Vuicho, and one of the best sommeliers in the world, Gerard Basset. All these men remain dear friends.

SERVES: 2
PREPARATION TIME: 20 MINUTES PLUS 5 HOURS INFUSION TIME
COOKING TIME: 10–15 MINUTES

Confit
20ml olive oil
10 baby onions, peeled
1 banana shallot, peeled and diced
3 baby leeks, sliced 2mm thick
1 red pepper, deseeded and diced
1 green pepper, deseeded and diced
2 baby fennel bulbs, diced
80g mushrooms, quartered
2 star anise
½ vanilla pod, halved lengthways
8 garlic cloves, halved and core removed
9 whole black peppercorns
10–20 coriander seeds

2 bay leaves
juice and zest of 1 lemon
juice and zest of 1 orange
150–200ml extra-virgin olive oil
4 sprigs fresh thyme, stalks removed, chopped
8 fresh basil leaves, torn
5g fresh coriander, chopped
1 beef tomato, diced
For the fish
20ml olive oil
4 fillets lemon sole
juice of ½ lemon
sea salt and freshly ground black pepper

1. First, make the confit. Heat some olive oil in a frying pan and fry the baby onions for 3–4 minutes. Add the shallot, leeks, red and green peppers, fennel and mushrooms, and cook for 3 minutes.

2. Add the star anise, vanilla, garlic, peppercorns, coriander seeds, bay leaves, and the zest and juices of the lemon and orange. When hot, remove from the heat and stir in the extra-virgin olive oil. Set the pan aside, covered, for 5 hours to infuse.

3. Return the pan to the heat and bring almost to boiling point but do not boil. Remove from the heat, and add the thyme, basil, fresh coriander and tomato. Stir to combine and set aside while you cook the fish.

4. Put a little olive oil in a frying pan on a high heat. Season the sole fillets. Place in the hot pan, squeeze over the lemon juice and fry for 3–4 minutes on each side, or until coloured.

5. Turn the vegetable confit on to a hot plate, lay the fish on the top and serve immediately.

The confit can be kept in a jar for up to 10 days.

Pork Mince Croquettes with Sweet Chilli Dip

Choose the piece of pork you want and get your butcher to mince it for you. I always go for outdoor reared pork or organic pork as it has such good flavour.

SERVES: 4–6
PREPARATION TIME: 10 MINUTES
COOKING TIME: 10 MINUTES

1 tablespoon olive oil
600g minced pork, chopped
small bunch fresh thyme, stalks removed and chopped
small bunch fresh coriander, chopped
1 teaspoon medium curry powder
a few drops Tabasco
1 teaspoon Dijon mustard

2 small onions, peeled and finely chopped
2 garlic cloves, peeled and sliced
300g cooked potato, mashed
1 medium egg white
300g choux paste (see page 208)
500ml olive oil for frying
100ml sweet chilli sauce
salt and freshly ground black pepper

1. Heat the tablespoon of oil in a frying pan. Pan-fry the pork, herbs, curry powder, Tabasco, mustard, onions and garlic for 3 minutes, or until the pork is cooked, and then add the mashed potato and seasoning. Stir to combine.

2. Turn the pork into a large bowl and combine with the egg white and choux paste. Form into small croquettes, keeping your hands wet so it doesn't stick.

3. Heat the 500ml olive oil in a frying pan and fry the croquettes until crispy and there is no pink meat remaining.

4. Serve the hot croquettes with the chilli sauce.

This dish works equally well with minced beef or chicken. Make sure the oil for deep frying is at the right temperature – 180°C. If you drop a bit of mix in and it colours very quickly then it is too hot. When the croquettes start floating, they're ready.

Chou Farci

Stuffed cabbage, or chou farci, *is one of my old favourite family recipes that I was bought up on. It is good hearty food, made with finesse but also retains a traditional home-cooked feel.*

SERVES: 4
PREPARATION TIME: 12–15 MINUTES
COOKING TIME: 25 MINUTES

2 Savoy cabbages
10ml olive oil
Stuffing
150g lean pork, chopped
150g pork fat, chopped
25g chicken livers, trimmed and finely
 chopped
½ garlic clove, peeled and crushed
2 tablespoons flat-leaf parsley, chopped

10g fresh breadcrumbs
25ml dry white wine
2 teaspoons brandy
1 small egg, beaten
salt and freshly ground black pepper
To serve
⅓ quantity proper tomato sauce
 (see page 220)

1. Remove twelve unblemished outer leaves from the cabbages, wash thoroughly and blanch for 1 minute in boiling water to soften. Remove with a slotted spoon and set aside.

2. To make the stuffing, mince together the pork, pork fat, livers, garlic, parsley, breadcrumbs, wine, brandy and egg. Combine thoroughly, then season and stir to combine. Divide the stuffing into four portions.

3. Take one cabbage leaf, drizzle with oil and in the centre mound up one portion of the stuffing. Cover with two more cabbage leaves. Put the parcel on a square of doubled cling film. Pull the four corners in together to make a tight parcel and then twist so that the cling film tightens around the stuffing, gathering it into a ball. Repeat with the remaining leaves to make four balls in total.

4. Place the cabbage balls, in their cling film, in a steamer over boiling water. Cover with a lid and steam for 20 minutes.

5. To serve, unwrap the cabbage balls from the cling film and place each in the centre of a bowl. The filling should be hot through and there should be no pink meat remaining; if not, return to the steamer. Heat the tomato sauce gently and pour carefully around each ball. Serve immediately.

Tuna Steak Tartare Rapido

This is an alternative to the classic steak tartare, as long as you use fresh tuna. When I prepare this dish I make sure that the fish is as fresh as possible and I make it in the most hygienic conditions. It is also great as a starter.

SERVES: 2
PREPARATION TIME: 15–10 MINUTES
COOKING TIME: 1–2 MINUTES
MARINATING TIME: 1–2 HOURS

200g fresh tuna steaks, skinned
1 teaspoon Tabasco
2 tablespoons lemon juice
1 tablespoon baby capers
salt and freshly ground pepper
2 jumbo gherkins, finely diced
20g onion, peeled and chopped
20g shallots, peeled and chopped
1 baguette

¼ avocado, diced
5g fresh chervil, roughly chopped
5g fresh chives, roughly chopped
½ teaspoon medium curry powder
1 teaspoon English mustard
50ml mayonnaise
2 tablespoons olive oil, for frying
2 quail's eggs

1. Mince the fresh tuna and turn into a bowl with the Tabasco, lemon juice, capers, seasoning, gherkins, onion and shallots. Cover and leave to marinate in the fridge for 1–2 hours. (If you do not have a mincer, blitz the tuna briefly in a blender or food processor or chop it finely.)

2. Preheat the oven to 130°C/Fan 110°C/Gas 1.

3. Five minutes before serving, put the bread into the preheated oven to warm. Or dry fry to toast before serving.

4. Stir the avocado and herbs into the tuna and its marinade. In a separate bowl, mix the curry powder with the mustard and mayonnaise. Turn into the bowl of tuna and combine thoroughly.

5. In a frying pan, heat the olive oil and fry the quail's eggs immediately before serving. This should only take a minute so don't use too high a heat.

6. Take the baguette out of the oven then carefully slice it in half at an angle. Place the tuna on to each slice and top this with a quail's egg.

If you prefer, you can cook the tuna before you mince it: seal it first in a very hot pan for about 4 seconds on each side.

Minute-poached Salmon and Gorgonzola Rigatoni

This is a fantastic dish and is quick to make, so it's perfect for unexpected visitors like my daughter Christina and her band. If you don't like salmon, this works equally well with another oily fish or chicken.

SERVINGS: 2
PREPARATION TIME: 15 MINUTES
COOKING TIME: 45 MINUTES

3 tablespoons extra-virgin olive oil
1 onion, peeled and diced
2 banana shallots, peeled and diced
2 x 400g cans chopped tomatoes
1 teaspoon caster sugar
1 sprig fresh thyme, stalks removed
2 garlic cloves, peeled, halved and core removed, crush one and keep the other whole
400g dry rigatoni pasta

150g Gorgonzola cheese
400g boneless, skinless salmon fillet, gently poached in 200ml vegetable nage (see page 200) or pan-fried in olive oil for 2 minutes on each side in a covered pan
salt and freshly ground black pepper
25g baby spinach leaves
10g fresh basil leaves, torn
3 tablespoons double cream

1. First, make the sauce. Heat 2 tablespoons olive oil in a medium-sized frying pan and gently cook the onion and shallots until translucent. Add the tomatoes, sugar and thyme, and simmer for 20 minutes or until reduced. Add the crushed garlic clove.

2. While the sauce is cooking, bring a large pan of salted water to the boil, to which about 1 tablespoon olive oil has been added, and add the pasta. Cook according to the directions on the packet until al dente.

3. Drain, retaining some cooking liquid to keep the pasta moist.

4. Add the cheese to the tomato sauce. Be careful not to cook the cheese, just warm it through. Flake the salmon into the sauce and season to taste.

5. Tip the tomato sauce into a large bowl and fold in the warm pasta, followed by the spinach and basil.

6. Pour the pasta and sauce mixture back into the pan, then stir in the cream and add the garlic clove to infuse with flavour.

7. Gently heat through and check the seasoning. Serve immediately.

Keep the Gorgonzola out of the fridge for 1 hour before introducing to the dish.

Sweet Curried Seafood Stew with Beer

This medley of seafood is one of my favourites, especially since I'm a Frenchman. I use a lot of fresh vegetables and herbs here to give it lots of flavour, and only a hint of curry. It was inspired by Frau Helga Kesster who, in my eyes, makes some of the best curries in the world.

SERVES: 6
PREPARATION TIME: 25 MINUTES
COOKING TIME: 1 HOUR

30ml olive oil, for frying
1 onion, chopped
2 sticks celery, chopped
2 banana shallots, chopped
1 large leek, chopped
handful fresh thyme, stalks removed
1 bay leaf
½ teaspoon medium curry powder
½ teaspoon caster sugar
600ml beer (preferably Leffe)
100g monkfish, cut into large cubes
6 baby squid
100g cod, cut into large cubes
100g smoked haddock, cut into large cubes

6 raw tiger prawns
50g salmon, cut into large cubes
500g mussels and clams, washed in cold water and with the beards removed
100ml double cream
200g pancetta, diced
50g tomatoes, chopped
2 tablespoons fresh mixed herbs, chopped (basil, chervil, tarragon, parsley)
Garlic croûtons
60ml olive oil
3 garlic cloves, peeled and finely chopped
2–3 slices bread, crusts removed and cut into 4–5mm cubes

1. Preheat the oven to 200°C/Fan 180°C/Gas 6.

2. Heat the olive oil in a large frying pan and gently cook the onion, celery, shallots and leek with the thyme and bay leaf over a low heat until softened.

3. Add the curry powder, sugar and beer, bring to the boil and simmer steadily until the liquid has reduced by half. Add the monkfish and squid, and cook for 1 minute. Add the remaining fish and shellfish. Simmer for 10 minutes. Turn down the heat and add the cream – do not allow it to boil.

4. To make the garlic croûtons, in another small pan, heat the 60ml olive oil, add the garlic and cook gently for 10 minutes. Remove from the heat. Dip the bread cubes in the garlicky oil and then place on a baking tray. Bake in the preheated oven for about 10–15 minutes, or until dry and crisp.

5. In a separate frying pan, fry the pancetta until crisp. Remove with a slotted spoon and add to the fish.

6. In the same pan, add a little more olive oil and fry the tomatoes until soft. Add to the fish together with the mixed herbs.

7. Taste the stew and adjust the seasoning. Finally, garnish with the garlic croûtons and serve immediately, accompanied by diced potatoes.

Strawberry and Lemongrass Skewers

This is a very simple and quick recipe to make, perfect for barbeques. Use fresh summer strawberries threaded on to lemongrass skewers, which can be the fresh variety or dried in pots. Don't forget to prick the lemongrass with a small knife to release the juices and try to use the largest strawberries as possible, keeping the stalks on. By not taking them off, the juices of the strawberries are not released too quickly.

SERVES: 4
PREPARATION TIME: 10 MINUTES
COOKING TIME: 8 MINUTES

4 sticks lemongrass
20 large English strawberries
100ml runny honey
½ teaspoon black pepper, finely ground
1 teaspoon sunflower oil
juice of 1–1½ lemons

To serve
8 scoops vanilla ice-cream
4 sprigs mint

1. Preheat the oven to 220°C/Fan 200°C/Gas 7.

2. Push each lemongrass stalk through the centre of 5 of the strawberries. Arrange on an ovenproof dish.

3. In a saucepan, heat the honey, black pepper and oil for 1 minute. Remove from the heat. Add the lemon juice, stir to combine and pour over the kebabs.

4. Cut out 4 foil circles with a 9cm diameter. Place a skewer in the centre of each one and baste with the marinade. Fold two wide edges together and crimp to make an open parcel so the liquid stays inside.

5. Place the dish on a baking tray and cook in the preheated oven for 7–8 minutes.

6. Remove from the oven, carefully open the foil and roll back the edges to form an oval bowl. Place a scoop or two of ice-cream on the hot strawberries, decorate with the mint and serve immediately.

Choose firm strawberries. You can vary the recipe with other seasonal fruit, such as plums, bananas, apricots etc.

Crème Légère Monique

This is one of my mother's favourite recipes. A good crème légère needs care when it is made and you need to use fresh milk, eggs and plump juicy sultanas or prunes. Make sure not to overheat it when you cook or this dessert may curdle.

SERVES: 10–12
PREPARATION TIME: 10–15 MINUTES
FREEZER/CHILLING TIME: 2–4 HOURS, OR IDEALLY OVERNIGHT
COOKING TIME: 35–45 MINUTES

150g sultanas
50ml brandy
100g granulated sugar
2 tablespoons cold water

4 medium egg yolks
9 medium whole eggs
375g soft brown sugar
1 litre full fat milk

1. First, in a saucepan cover the sultanas with cold water, bring to the boil and simmer gently for about 1 hour. As the water evaporates, keep adding more, ensuring that the sultanas remain covered.

2. When the sultanas have plumped up, take them out and leave them to cool. Allow the remaining liquid to reduce. Remove from the heat, add the brandy and set aside, covered, for 15 minutes.

3. Preheat the oven to 130°C/Fan 110°C/Gas 1.

4. In a separate pan, add the sugar to the reduced liquid, and slowly heat until the sugar has dissolved (there should be no grittiness when it is stirred with a spoon). Bring to the boil and cook until caramel in colour, roughly 2–3 minutes. Pour into 10–12 x 150ml pudding moulds.

5. Top each mould with 10g sultanas and leave to cool.

6. Meanwhile, whisk together the egg yolks, whole eggs and soft brown sugar until a ribbon forms from the whisk.

7. Pour the milk into another pan and bring to the boil. Once it has boiled, allow it to cool slightly, then whisk in the egg mixture. Skim the foam from the mixture and then pour into the moulds over the sultanas.

8. Cook the moulds in a bain-marie (a roasting tin filled halfway up with water) in the preheated oven for 35–45 minutes or until just set.

9. Remove from the oven but allow to cool slowly in the bain-marie for 10 minutes before chilling in the fridge for at least 2–4 hours or ideally overnight. Serve chilled.

You will achieve the right texture if you take them out of the oven when they are still wobbly like jelly.

Bitter Chocolate and Honeycomb Parfait

This recipe requires a good quality chocolate containing at least 70 per cent cocoa solids and I use a Fairtrade one. To get a smooth texture I use egg yolks and not the egg whites because they tend to make the mixture tough. This is one of my good friend and right-hand chef-in-command Wesley Smalley's favourite recipes at the White Horse in Harpenden. You will need a cook's thermometer.

SERVES: 4
PREPARATION TIME: 15 MINUTES
FREEZER/CHILLING TIME: 3–4 HOURS OR OVERNIGHT
COOKING TIME: 10 MINUTES

30g caster sugar
12ml liquid glucose
1 teaspoon runny honey
1 teaspoon water
½ teaspoon bicarbonate of soda (sifted)

25g good-quality bitter chocolate, 70 per cent cocoa solids, broken in pieces
80ml stock syrup (see page 235)
150ml whipping cream
2 large egg yolks

1. Place four mousse rings, 60mm x 45mm, on a greaseproof-paper-lined tray and place into the freezer until needed. If you don't have four small mousse rings, 1 large jelly mould will do.

2. Place the sugar, glucose, honey and water in a saucepan, bring to the boil and then cook to a light caramel, roughly 5–6 minutes.

3. When pale and golden brown, remove the pan from the heat and stir in the bicarbonate of soda, which will rise up the pan. Without knocking the air out, carefully pour this mix on to a baking tray lined with greaseproof paper and leave to cool.

4. When cool, melt the chocolate in a bain-marie and pour over the honeycomb, coating it well. Allow to cool.

5. Using a cook's thermometer bring the stock syrup to 120°C and then take off the heat.

6. Meanwhile, whip the cream in a bowl to soft peaks. And, in another bowl, whisk the egg yolks with an electric whisk or beater until they form thick ribbons when the whisk is held up. Carefully fold the cream and stock syrup into the egg yolks.

7. Smash the chocolate honeycomb into pieces and fold this into the parfait. Fill the mousse rings with the parfait and level the tops.

9. Put back into the freezer for 3–4 hours or overnight. Serve straight from the freezer.

If you are short of time, use 50g ready-made honeycomb instead of making the caramel.

Exotic Fruit Ice Parfait

Here's a really great dessert bursting with tropical flavour, introduced to me by my greatest friend, Marco Pierre White. This is one of those ideal recipes: they can be made in advance as they freeze well.

SERVES: 16
PREPARATION TIME: 10–15 MINUTES
FREEZER/CHILLING TIME: 4 HOURS OR OVERNIGHT
COOKING TIME: 3–5 MINUTES

800g mixed fresh fruit, freshly prepared
    (pineapple, kiwi, mango, passion fruit
    and pomegranate, or use 800g of your
    favourite fruit)
450g caster sugar
2 star anise
1 vanilla pod, halved lengthways

juice of 4 limes
juice of 1 orange
100ml Malibu or rum (optional)
700ml double cream
3 medium egg whites
pinch salt

1. Place the fruit in a large saucepan, add 350g of the sugar and bring to the boil. Cook until the fruit collapses into a pulp. Turn down the heat, add the star anise and vanilla pod and leave to simmer gently for 5 minutes.

2. Remove from the heat and leave to cool quickly in the fridge on a flat tray. When cool, add the lime and orange juice, and the Malibu or rum (if using).

3. Half-whip the double cream and, in a separate bowl, whisk the egg whites to stiff peaks with a tiny pinch of salt. Add the remaining sugar to the egg whites, a little at a time, and whisk after each addition to form a meringue. Fold in the cream.

4. When the pulp is completely cold, fold carefully into the meringue and then spoon gently into 16 dariole moulds.

5. Cover each mould with cling film and freeze for at least 4 hours or ideally overnight. Serve straight from the freezer.

Never bang your whisk after mixing the meringue otherwise you will lose air. When you introduce the cream, make sure it is well chilled and only half whipped.

Tartes Fines with Pineapple and Chilli

This is one of my favourite dessert recipes combining chilli with Tabsco, pineapple, ginger and honey. It looks stunning when finished and is great served with crème fraîche.

SERVES: 2
PREPARATION TIME: 25-30 MINUTES
FREEZING/CHILLING TIME: 30 MINUTES
COOKING TIME: 20–25 MINUTES
MARINATING TIME: 12 HOURS OR OVERNIGHT

1 small pineapple, peeled
100ml lemon juice, roughly 3–4 large
   lemons or 5–6 small ones
60ml rum
150ml runny honey
20g fresh ginger, peeled and sliced
1 red chilli, deseeded and cut in half
1 vanilla pod, halved lengthways

1 teaspoon Tabasco
100ml water
100g ready-made puff pastry
icing sugar
To serve
1 sprig fresh mint
100ml crème fraîche
1 teaspoon lemon juice

1. Cut the pineapple into slices 2mm thick, and remove the hard central core.

2. In a dish, combine the lemon juice, rum, honey, ginger, chilli, vanilla, Tabasco and water. Add the pineapple and marinate for 12 hours in the fridge.

3. Roll out the puff pastry and cut out two discs to roughly the size of a side plate. Open-freeze for 30 minutes.

4. Preheat the oven to 180°C/Fan 160°C/Gas 4.

5. Drain the pineapple, reserving the marinade, and set aside. Pour the marinade into a saucepan and on a gentle heat reduce to a syrup. Pass through a sieve and cool.

6. Take the pastry out of the freezer and put the discs on a baking tray lined with greaseproof paper. Cover with another sheet of greaseproof paper and then put another baking tray on top to prevent the pastry rising. Bake in the preheated oven for 5 minutes.

7. Remove from the oven. Place the trays on the floor, put an old newspaper on top, laid out flat, and stand in the centre so that your weight flattens the pastry. Return to the hot oven and bake for 7 minutes.

8. Remove from the oven, and lift off both the second baking tray and the greaseproof paper. Arrange the reserved pineapple slices on the pastry circles, drizzle with the syrup and dust with icing sugar. Return to the oven for 8–10 minutes, or until bubbling.

9. Meanwhile, chop the mint and add to the crème fraîche with a squeeze of lemon.

10. Serve the tartes hot from the oven, accompanied by the crème fraîche.

AFTERNOON TEA

Ham and Cheese Beignets
Deep-fried Smoked Salmon Scotch Eggs
Baked Glazed Apples
My Own Eton Mess
Rum Babas
Swan Meringues
Home-made Fudge
Warm Cherry Clafoutis
Caramelised Banana Splits with
 Rum and Chocolate Sauce
Fox's Mint Bonbon Tuile Biscuit
Rocher
Chocolate Macaroon Yo-Yos

Ham and Cheese Beignets

A delicious snack or starter, this is made from only a few basic ingredients. The secret to this recipe is to make sure that the frying temperature is right and the cheese is encased well in the centre of the choux pastry. Serve with a salad of your choice.

SERVES: 6
PREPARATION TIME: 45 MINUTES
COOKING TIME: 7 MINUTES

240g ham hock, cooked and chopped
1 large egg white
salt and freshly ground black pepper
150ml olive oil
4 tablespoons fresh flat-leaf parsley, chopped

juice of 1 lemon
300g choux paste (about ½ quantity see page 208)
125g Brie, cubed

1. Heat a deep-fat fryer or pan of oil to 180°C.

2. Put the ham and egg white into a blender or food processor, and blitz to combine.

3. Season, and slowly mix in the olive oil – blitzing all the time. When it has reached a paste consistency, add the parsley and the lemon juice.

4. Fold the ham mixture into the choux paste and then stir in the cubes of Brie.

5. Form into balls using 2 soup spoons and carefully drop into the deep-fat fryer. Fry for 4–5 minutes each.

6. Remove from the oil and drain on kitchen paper. Repeat with the remaining mixture. The recipe will make 24 beignets.

When a beignet floats, it is a sign that it is ready. If using a pan to heat the oil, it should only be a third full.

Deep-fried Smoked Salmon Scotch Eggs

This dish, very much inspired by traditional Scotch eggs, requires a little bit of technique to get the shape right.

SERVES: 4
PREPARATION TIME: 15 MINUTES
CHILLING TIME: 1 HOUR
COOKING TIME: 2–3 MINUTES FOR EACH EGG

400g smoked salmon, roughly chopped
½ shallot, peeled and roughly chopped
4 medium egg yolks
lemon juice
2 teaspoons fresh chervil, chopped
4 medium eggs, hard-boiled and peeled

seasoned flour
handful sesame seeds
Egg wash
1–2 medium egg yolks
1 teaspoon cold water
pinch salt

1. In a food processor or blender, blitz together the salmon, shallot, egg yolks and a squeeze of lemon juice until smooth.

2. Place in a bowl, stir in the chervil and chill in the fridge for about 1 hour.

3. Heat a deep-fat fryer or pan of oil to 190°C. Make the egg wash by beating together the ingredients.

4. Take 2 serving spoons and cover one with cling film. Place an even quantity f smoked salmon in each spoon. Place one of the hard-boiled eggs in the middle of one spoon, then place the other spoon on top.

5. Make sure the egg is enclosed by the salmon paste and then wrap the cling film around until it is covered evenly.

6. Remove the parcel from the cling film and roll in seasoned flour, followed by the egg wash. Finally, coat in sesame seeds.

7. Repeat with the remaining eggs.

8. Fry in the deep-fat fryer for 2–3 minutes each and then drain on kitchen paper. Serve hot with mixed salad leaves.

For a less expensive option, use smoked trout. If chervil is unavailable, use dill or flat-leaf parsley.

Baked Glazed Apples

A great combination of apple, goat's cheese and foie gras with a hint of cumin seeds. It can be served hot or cold.

SERVES: 10
PREPARATION TIME: 15 MINUTES
CHILLING TIME (OPTIONAL): 12 HOURS
COOKING TIME: 15–20 MINUTES

10 Bramley or Granny Smith apples
pinch cumin seeds
2 teaspoons caster sugar, and more
   for sprinkling

400g foie gras
salt and freshly ground black pepper
200–250g log goat's cheese (e.g. St Maure)

1. With a sharp knife, cut a slice off the very top of the apples and scoop out the flesh, being careful not to damage the skins.

2. Remove and discard the core and pips. Chop the flesh and cook in a small amount of water, roughly 1 tablespoon, until soft to make a compote. Add a pinch of cumin seeds and a pinch of sugar.

3. Heat a large frying pan. Cut the foie gras into 10 even pieces and season with salt, pepper and sugar. When the pan is very hot, cook the pieces on each side for 15 seconds. Remove with a slotted spoon and set aside to cool.

4. Preheat the oven to 160°C/Fan 140°C/Gas 3. Cut the goat's cheese into 10 portions, which should be roughly the same size as the cavities in the apples.

5. Fill the bottom quarter of each apple with the compote. Then add a piece of the foie gras, a drizzle of the fat from the pan, followed by a slice of the cheese. If there is enough room around the edges of the cheese, pack with more apple compote. (You can add fresh herbs at this stage for more flavour if you wish – try a small sprig of thyme or a bay leaf in each.)

6. Bake the apples in the preheated oven for 10–15 minutes. Preheat the grill.

7. Remove the apples from the oven and allow to cool slightly, roughly 5 minutes. Sprinkle with sugar and then glaze the tops, either under the preheated grill or with a culinary blowtorch.

8. The apples can be served either hot or cold. If serving cold, chill for at least 12 hours.

Granny Smith apples are best for their sharpness and texture.

My Own Eton Mess

From what is supposed to be a mess, what a great tradtional British dessert. You can't beat the flavour and texture of British strawberries sweetened with honey.

SERVES: 6
PREPARATION TIME: 20 MINUTES
COOKING TIME: 3 HOURS

140ml thick honey
5 large egg whites
pinch salt

600ml double cream
1 quantity coconut cream (see page 237)
700g strawberries, hulled and sliced

1. Preheat the oven to 100°C/Fan 90°C/Gas ¼, and line 2 baking trays with baking parchment.

2. Warm the honey in a saucepan until almost boiling. Remove from the heat.

3. Using an electric whisk, whisk the egg whites together in a bowl with the salt to stiff peaks. Add the hot honey very gradually, a few drops at a time, and whisk until it leaves a thick, fluffy, glossy trail when the whisk is lifted.

4. Using 2 soup spoons to shape them, spoon 6 meringues on to each baking tray. Bake in the preheated oven for 3 hours or until dry and crisp. Remove from the oven and leave to cool for a few minutes.

5. Combine the double cream and coconut cream and half whip them together to thicken.

6. Roughly crush the warm meringues and quickly combine them with the strawberries and creams. Be careful not to stir the cream with the warm meringue too much or the raised temperature will cause the cream to separate. Pile into a glass serving bowl or individual glasses. Serve immediately.

If time is short, use store-bought meringues. Before using, chill the strawberries in the freezer until they are cold but not frozen. For a bit of variation, add some toasted flaked almonds at the last minute.

Rum Babas

When I was a baker as a young teenager, I remember being in charge of plunging the baba in the warm rum. I used to really feel the effects of the alcohol vapours. This is a classic dish to which I've added my own touch. Steeped in a rum-based syrup and then filled with crème patisserie, it is worth the effort. You could also add a little seasonal fruit of your choice. You will need 10 dariole moulds for this recipe.

SERVES: 10
PREPARATION TIME: 1 HOUR
COOKING TIME: 20 MINUTES

plain flour, for dusting
150ml milk
35g fresh yeast
500g strong plain flour, sifted
1 teaspoon salt
60g caster sugar

6 medium eggs
200g unsalted butter, softened, plus extra
   for greasing
2 quantities stock syrup (500ml; see
   page 235) made with rum
half-quantity crème pâtissière (see page 236)

1. Preheat the oven to 180°C/Fan 160°C/Gas 4. Grease 10 dariole moulds with butter and dust each with a little flour.

2. Heat the milk in a pan until tepid, then remove from the heat and stir in the yeast.

3. In a bowl, combine the flour, salt and sugar. Add the eggs one at a time, beating well until each is incorporated. Add the butter and then pour in the warm milk. Knead well.

4. Divide the mixture between the moulds, ensuring that they are only two thirds full so that the dough has room to rise. Let them prove for 30 minutes.

5. Bake on a baking tray in the preheated oven for 15–18 minutes, or until risen and golden brown. Leave in the tins to cool.

6. When cool, remove from the moulds and arrange on a deep metal tray. Chill in the fridge for roughly 20 minutes, until very cold (this will prevent them from breaking up when soaked later).

7. Heat the stock syrup in a large pan and, when hot, pour over the cold babas. Leave to soak for 5–8 minutes or until all the syrup has been absorbed, turning once to ensure an even soaking.

8. Cut the babas in half horizontally, fill with crème pâtissière and serve.

Take care that the milk is only lukewarm; the yeast must not be heated up before baking.

Swan Meringues

This is one of the most therapeutic dishes to make. It is certainly worth the time and effort, plus it can be made in advance. I will never forget making this on my daughter Christina's first birthday.

MAKES: 15 SWANS
PREPARATION TIME: 30 MINUTES, PLUS DRYING TIME OF 24–36 HOURS

5 large egg whites, roughly 200ml
200g caster sugar
pinch salt
2 tablespoons cornflour, sifted
200g icing sugar, sifted

10g bitter chocolate
vanilla ice-cream
selection of red fruits (eg, raspberries, strawberries and redcurrants) or spiced mixed berries (see page 4)

1. Using an electric whisk, whisk the egg whites until they form stiff peaks. Add the caster sugar and a pinch of salt continue whisking until the whites are glossy, very thick and hold their shape.

2. Sift the cornflour and icing sugar over the whites and, using a spatula, fold in carefully and thoroughly, leaving no lumps.

3. Line a baking tray with greaseproof paper. Carefully transfer a third of the meringue into a piping bag fitted with a plain nozzle. Pipe the swan's necks on to the paper with one beak on each end, so that if one breaks off, you can use the other. It doesn't matter if the quantity of meringue produces more necks than you need since it is difficult to remove them from the greaseproof paper without breaking and this will give you some room for error. Turn the remaining meringue into a piping bag fitted with a star-shaped nozzle. Pipe half of the mixture to make wings for one side using a left to right motion and the other half using a right to left motion.

4. Leave to dry in a cool dry place (not the fridge) for 24–36 hours.

5. When dry, remove from the greaseproof paper using a palette knife, being careful not to break the meringue.

6. Melt the chocolate in a bain-marie or in a bowl over a pan of boiling water, making sure that the bottom does not touch the water. Dip a cocktail stick into the chocolate, then on to the swan's head to make a dot of chocolate for the eye.

7. Have a cold serving plate to hand and scoop out the ice-cream to form a ball and place in the centre of the plate.

8. Carefully press the swan's wings on to the ice-cream, then add the neck and head.

9. Decorate with the raspberries, strawberries and redcurrants. Serve immediately.

The meringue shapes can be made in advance and will keep for a couple of weeks in an airtight tin.

Home made Fudge

This just melts in your mouth. It is simple to make and the secret is to whisk it well when it reaches the correct temperature. Store in airtight containers. You will need a chef's thermometer for this recipe.

MAKES: 40 PIECES
PREPARATION TIME: 5 MINUTES
CHILLING TIME: 6 HOURS
COOKING TIME: 10–20 MINUTES

50g unsalted butter, plus extra for greasing
4 tablespoons water
2 tablespoons golden syrup or honey

450g granulated sugar
8 tablespoons sweetened full-cream
  condensed milk

1. Grease an 18cm square tin with butter.

2. Put the 50g butter, water, syrup or honey, sugar and condensed milk in a large heavy-based pan. Stir over a gentle heat until the sugar dissolves.

3. Bring to the boil and boil steadily, stirring from time to time, until it reaches 119°C.

4. Remove from the heat and beat well with an electric whisk until it starts to turn cloudy.

5. Pour into the prepared tin and allow to cool for 6 hours.

6. When cold, cut into squares and serve, or keep in an airtight tin for 3–4 days.

For vanilla fudge, scrape out the seeds from half a vanilla pod and add them at step 2. For rum- or brandy-flavoured fudge, add 2–3 tablespoons at step 2. For almond fudge, sprinkle a thin layer of very dry flaked toasted almonds over the bottom of the tin at step 1. At step 5 alternate layers of fudge with sprinkles of almonds, ending with a final layer of fudge.

Warm Cherry Clafoutis

This is a wonderful summertime dessert and is well worth the effort of stoning the cherries. I use the wonderful British home-grown cherries as they cook well and burst with flavour. This recipe is nearly as good as the one made by the mother of my childhood best friend Jean Louis Farjot from Brittany, also a great chef.

SERVES: 3–4
PREPARATION TIME: 10–15 MINUTES
COOKING TIME: 45 MINUTES

20ml kirsch
750g ripe cherries, with stones removed
6 medium eggs
pinch salt
100g self-raising flour, sifted

90g caster sugar
250ml milk
1 x 2g sachet vanilla sugar, or 2–3 drops vanilla essence
icing sugar and cocoa powder, for sprinkling

1. Preheat the oven to 200°C/Fan 180°C/Gas 6, and grease a 22cm x 30cm china flan dish. Pour the kirsch over the cherries and leave to infuse while you make the batter.

2. Beat the eggs and the salt together, add the flour and sugar, and stir to combine. Pour in the milk gradually, a little at a time, stirring constantly. Stir in the vanilla sugar or essence.

3. Sprinkle the flan dish with some icing sugar and cocoa powder, and then pour in the batter. Scatter the infused cherries and the kirsch across the top – they will sink in.

4. Bake in the preheated oven for 45 minutes or until set.

5. Serve warm, sprinkled with icing sugar.

This recipe is equally good with other seasonal fruit, like blueberries or stoned plums. You can also serve this with warm caramel or chocolate sauce. Add a tiny touch of yeast to the recipe to inflate the mix. Coating the flan dish with unsalted butter, icing sugar and cocoa powder gives extra crust, flavours and colour.

Caramelised Banana Splits with Rum and Chocolate Sauce

This recipe is a wonderful medley of flavours and tropical notes with a hint of spice. Best eaten warm. Definitely better than using raw bananas.

SERVES: 2
PREPARATION TIME: 10 MINUTES
COOKING TIME: 25–30 MINUTES

2 large bananas, almost ripe
1 vanilla pod
100g caster sugar
100ml water
100ml double cream
1 star anise
100ml rum

30g bitter chocolate, 70 per cent cocoa
    solids grated
To serve
crème fraîche, mascarpone or double cream
freshly grated nutmeg or sifted cocoa
    powder, for dusting

1. Preheat the oven to 140°C/Fan 120°C/Gas 1.

2. Roll the unpeeled bananas on a hard surface to soften them. Prick a hole in the top. Roll the vanilla pod in your hands to soften and then cut in half lengthways and cut one of the halves in half again. Insert a quarter pod into each banana. Place in an ovenproof dish and bake in the preheated oven for 15–18 minutes.

3. Meanwhile, make a caramel sauce by heating the sugar and water in a pan until it starts to colour, roughly 10 minutes. Stir in half of the double cream and then add the star anise and half the rum.

4. Remove the bananas from the oven, split them open down the centre lengthwise and, still in their skins, pour over the sauce. Return to the hot oven to bake for a further 10 minutes.

5. Meanwhile, make a quick chocolate sauce by melting the grated chocolate with the remaining cream and rum in a bain-marie or in a bowl over a pan of hot water, making sure the bottom of the bowl does not touch the water.

6. Place the bananas in a serving dish. Pour over the chocolate sauce, top with crème fraîche, mascarpone or double cream, and a dusting of nutmeg or cocoa powder. Serve immediately.

For best results, use firm, nearly ripe bananas.

Fox's Mint Bonbon Tuile Biscuit

As with all great things, I happened upon this fantastic dish by mistake! Fox's Mints are the English equivalent of Betise de Cambrai in France – another recipe which was also created by mistake. Instead of being served as a biscuit, the tuiles can be crushed and sprinkled on chocolate ice-cream.

MAKES: 15–20
PREPARATION TIME: 10 MINUTES
COOKING TIME: 3–5 MINUTES

70g Fox's mints, or any other clear boiled mint

1. Preheat the oven to 180°C/Fan 160°C/Gas 4.

2. Line a baking tray with baking parchment.

3. Blitz the mints in a food processor or blender until they turn into powder.

4. Sprinkle on to the tray, making sure that it is evenly spread and just covers the surface. Bake in the preheated oven for about 3–5 minutes or until melted.

5. Remove from the oven and leave on the tray to cool.

6. When cold, break into biscuit-size pieces.

When the mints have been blitzed, the powder must be used straightaway. When making the tuiles in humid or wet weather, store them in air-tight containers once cold. If you want, scatter with toasted or flaked almonds before baking.

Rocher

Light and fluffy pillows of meringue with a crispy outside and a soft marshmallow inside.

SERVES: 4
PREPARATION TIME: 15–25 MINUTES
COOKING TIME: 10–15 MINUTES

6 medium egg whites
pinch salt
30g caster sugar

250g icing sugar, sifted
100g flaked almonds
cocoa powder, for dusting

1. Preheat the oven to 140°C/Fan 120°C/Gas 1.

2. Using an electric whisk, beat together the egg whites and salt until they form stiff peaks. Carefully fold in the caster sugar and allow to stand for 10 minutes.

3. Line a baking tray with baking parchment, using a little oil underneath to keep the paper in place.

4. Gradually fold in the icing sugar and the almonds.

5. Using 2 teaspoons, one to pick up the meringue, the other one to scrape it off the first spoon, drop small amounts on the prepared baking tray. Sift over a little cocoa powder.

6. Bake in the preheated oven for 10–15 minutes or until crisp on the outside and soft in the middle.

7. Allow to cool on the tray. When cold, store in an airtight tin.

If wished, replace the ground almonds with the same quantity of desiccated coconut.

Chocolate Macaroon Yo-Yos

Rich and nutty, this is a must when you are entertaining children. The soft texture of the chocolate gives a sharp contrast to the homemade macroons.

MAKES: 10-12
PREPARATION TIME: 35 MINUTES, PLUS 25 MINUTES RESTING TIME
CHILLING TIME: 24 HOURS
COOKING TIME: 12 MINUTES

600g bitter chocolate, 70 per cent cocoa
   solids, broken into pieces
300ml glucose syrup
Macaroons
4 medium egg whites

225g icing sugar
25g caster sugar
225g ground almonds
¼ quantity crème pâtissière
   (see page 236)

1. To make the yo-yo 'string', melt the chocolate with the glucose syrup in a bain-marie or bowl over a pan of hot water, making sure that the bottom of the bowl does not touch the water.

2. When melted, stir together well. Pour on to some cling film, wrap up closely and chill for 24 hours.

3. To make the macaroons, whisk the egg whites until stiff. Sift together the sugars and fold carefully into the egg whites with the ground almonds to make an almond paste.

4. Leave to rest in the fridge for 25 minutes, covered loosely.

5. Preheat the oven to 180°C/Fan 160°C/Gas 4. Line a greased baking tray with baking parchment.

6. Turn the paste into a piping bag, fitted with a plain round 2.5cm nozzle. Pipe circles about 5–7cm diameter on to the parchment, 1–2cm apart. Bake in the preheated oven for about 10–12 minutes or until pale golden brown. Allow to cool on the tray.

7. Remove the chocolate from the fridge and, making sure your hands are cold, roll it out between your palms to make a string about 30cm long.

8. To serve, dab some crème pâtissière in the centre of the underside of each macaroon (there may be some left over). Place another on top to make a sandwich. Wind the chocolate string around the gap between the two macaroons, to resemble a yo-yo. Serve immediately or keep in an airtight container for up to a week.

Glucose syrup can be bought in supermarkets or chemists in small tubs.

DINNER

Honey Roast Pumpkin Soup
Monique Nibolitta Broth with Smoked Aioli
Cod Brandade Glazed with Red Peppers
Home-fed Mussels with Vanilla Piperade
Salmon en Croûte
Baked Aubergines with Baby Vegetables
Merlot-braised Oxtail with Pan-Fried
  Ricotta Gnocchi
The Best Beef and Cheese Lasagne
Slow Braised Honey and Cider Caramelised
  Pork Belly
Maman Novelli Chicken Fricassee
Hot Apricot Flan
White Chocolate and Passion
  Fruit Toffee Cup
Choco Pot Kahlúa
Kirsch, Mango and Pomegranate
  Rice Pudding

Honey Roast Pumpkin Soup

This is one of my favourite soups. It is filling and tasty and best served with slices of warm crusty French bread.

SERVES: 6–8
PREPARATION TIME: 10 MINUTES
COOKING TIME: 20–25 MINUTES

1kg fresh pumpkin, diced
50ml runny honey
80ml olive oil
500g onions, peeled and diced
4 bay leaves
5 sprigs fresh thyme, stalks removed
2 tablespoons white wine vinegar

450ml hot vegetable or chicken stock
½ litre double cream
salt and freshly ground black pepper
To serve
300g Red Leicester cheese, grated
crème fraîche

1. Preheat the oven to 180°C/Fan 160°C/Gas 4.

2. Coat the pumpkin with the honey in a roasting tray and bake in the preheated oven for 10–12 minutes, which will soften and caramelise it.

3. Meanwhile, heat the olive oil in a saucepan and add the onions, bay leaves, thyme and vinegar. Sweat gently for about 5–6 minutes, or until the onions are soft.

4. Add the pumpkin to the onions, together with the stock, and heat until almost at boiling point. Simmer steadily for about 20 minutes.

5. Remove and discard the bay leaves, and stir in the cream. Bring to the boil.

6. Once the soup has boiled, remove it from the heat and blitz in a blender or food processor. Pass through a sieve or strainer, and adjust the seasoning.

7. To serve, reheat in a clean pan. Ladle into bowls, sprinkle each with the cheese and top with a dollop of crème fraîche.

Butternut squash can be used as a substitute or even baby carrots.

Monique Nibolitta Broth with Smoked Aioli

Although this recipe has many ingredients, it is certainly worth making. It is packed with fresh, new season's vegetables and has the added subtle flavour of smoked ham. And it's even better when you eat it the next day.

SERVES: 4–6
PREPARATION TIME: 20–30 MINUTES
COOKING TIME: 50 MINUTES
INFUSION TIME: 1 HOUR

50g unsalted butter
100ml extra-virgin olive oil
2 shallots, diced
150g smoked pork belly, diced
40g canellini beans, cooked
2 baby turnips, cut into half
40g baby onions
40g chickpeas, cooked
1 carrot, diced
1 garlic clove, halved and core removed
1 sprig fresh thyme, stalk removed
2 bay leaves
salt and freshly ground black pepper
1 litre strong chicken stock
4 new potatoes
40g runner beans, sliced
40g broad beans

40g French beans, each cut into 3
1 celery stick, diced
3 baby leeks, sliced at an angle
40g garden peas
1 beef tomato, deseeded and diced
2 baby courgettes, each cut into 5 pieces
Aioli
2 medium egg yolks
juice of ½ lemon
1 teaspoon rock salt
½ teaspoon freshly ground black pepper
1 rounded teaspoon smoked paprika
½ teaspoon flat-leaf parsley, chopped
15 fresh basil leaves, torn
100–150ml olive oil, plus a little extra
   to serve

1. Heat the butter and olive oil in a wide, heavy-based pan. When hot, add the shallots, smoked pork belly, canellini beans, baby turnips, baby onions, chickpeas, carrot, garlic, thyme and bay leaves. Season.

2. Cook for 5–6 minutes, stirring from time to time.

3. Add the chicken stock, bring to the boil and simmer for 10–15 minutes.

4. Add the new potatoes, runner beans, broad beans, French beans, celery and baby leeks. Simmer for a further 25 minutes but do not allow to boil.

5. Remove the new potatoes with a slotted spoon and set aside to cool. Add the garden peas, tomato and courgettes.

6. Remove the pan from the heat and cover with a lid or foil, and leave undisturbed for 1 hour.

7. To make the aioli, skin the new potatoes when cool enough to handle, cut into small pieces and blitz in a blender or food processor. Add the egg yolks, lemon juice, salt, pepper, paprika and herbs, and blitz again. When blended, add 100ml olive oil. If needed, add the remaining oil – you should be aiming for a thick mayonnaise consistency. Adjust the seasoning.

8. To serve, reheat the broth until hot. Place about half a teaspoon of aioli in the bottom of each bowl. Drizzle a little extra olive oil around it, then ladle in the soup.

The green core of a garlic clove is indigestible, which is why it is always best to remove this.

Cod Brandade Glazed with Red Peppers

Use a tender fillet or loin of cod for this recipe. If the fish has the skin on, ask the fishmonger to skin it for you. When making the mashed potato, I use floury potatoes – ideal for mashing.

SERVES: 2
PREPARATION TIME: 15 MINUTES
COOKING TIME: 10 MINUTES

200g fresh raw cod fillet, skinned and flaked
8–10 fresh basil leaves, torn
1 garlic clove, peeled and chopped
10ml olive oil
lemon juice
100g hot mashed potatoes
20ml double cream
15g unsalted butter
½ teaspoon freshly grated nutmeg
1 red pepper, stalk removed, halved
  and deseeded

1 bay leaf
2 sprigs fresh thyme, stalks removed
salt and freshly ground black pepper
pinch caster sugar
2 tablespoons water
2 slices Cheddar cheese
pinch paprika
To serve
1 baguette

1. Preheat the oven to 200°C/Fan 180°C/Gas 4.

2. In a pestle and mortar, pound together the cod, basil, garlic, 1 teaspoon of the olive oil and a dash of lemon juice until it forms a paste. Alternatively, blitz in a blender or food processor.

3. Turn into a bowl and add the hot mashed potatoes, cream, butter and nutmeg. Beat to combine and set aside.

4. Heat the remaining olive oil in an ovenproof frying pan with a lid, and when very hot, add the red pepper, together with the bay leaf, thyme, seasoning and sugar.

5. Once the peppers have slightly browned, after 3–4 minutes, add the water to create steam. Cover immediately with a lid and put straight into the preheated oven for 2 minutes.

6. Remove from the oven and fill each pepper half with the fish paste. Cover with a thin slice of cheese and sprinkle with paprika.

7. Return to the hot oven and bake for a further 12 minutes. Preheat the grill until hot.

8. Cut the baguette in half lengthways and toast under the preheated grill until golden brown.

9. Serve the peppers with the toasted baguette.

This dish works equally
well if you use salmon
or haddock.

Home-fed Mussels with Vanilla Piperade

Plan this recipe forty-eight hours in advance. This will give you the time to rinse the mussels in clear water for 2 hours to remove the sand and then feed them on dry porridge flakes to increase their size. Carefully debeard the mussels with a sharp knife and scrape off any barnacles.

SERVES: 3–4
PREPARATION TIME: 20 MINUTES PLUS 48 HOURS SOAKING TIME
COOKING TIME: 40 MINUTES

1kg mussels
300g rolled oats
1 small aubergine, halved lengthways
salt and freshly ground black pepper
100ml olive oil
2 small onions, peeled and cut into thin shreds
3 garlic cloves, chopped and finely diced
4 sprigs fresh thyme, stalks removed
1 vanilla pod, halved lengthways
1 star anise
4 bay leaves
300ml white wine
½ teaspoon chilli powder

200g beef tomatoes, chopped
1 tablespoon tomato purée
1 teaspoon caster sugar
250g smoked bacon lardons, in 1cm dice
1 red pepper, deseeded and cut into thin strips
1 green pepper, deseeded and cut into thin strips
1 yellow pepper, deseeded and cut into thin strips
2 baby fennel, topped, tailed and cut into thin strips
10 fresh basil leaves

1. With a sharp knife, carefully remove the beard and barnacles from the mussel shells.

2. Cover the mussels with 3 litres cold water. Sprinkle on the oats and leave for 48 hours, stirring every 4–6 hours.

3. Drain the mussels and leave for 1 hour. Discard any that remain open.

4. Meanwhile, preheat the oven to 180°C/Fan 160°C/Gas 4. Place the aubergine halves on a baking tray, season and cover with foil. Bake in the preheated oven for 35 minutes or until the aubergine is soft. Remove from the oven and leave to cool. When cool enough to handle, scoop out the flesh, chop roughly and set aside.

5. Heat half the olive oil in a frying pan and when hot, add one of the onions, half of the garlic and the thyme, the vanilla, star anise and 1 bay leaf. Finally add the mussels. When the mixture hisses, add the white wine, then bring to the boil.

6. Remove from the heat and leave for 1 minute, then drain, reserving the cooking liquor. Remove and discard the vanilla and star anise.

7. Turn the mussels into a bowl and combine with about a third of the remaining olive oil. Cover with cling film and set aside.

8. Pour the cooking liquor from the mussels into a clean saucepan and reduce by a third.

9. Meanwhile, in a separate pan, heat the remaining olive oil and add the remaining onion, bay leaves, thyme, garlic and chilli powder. Then add the tomatoes, tomato purée and sugar.

10. Add the aubergine flesh and cook gently until it reduces to a pulp, roughly 10 minutes.

11. Meanwhile, heat a separate pan and when hot, add the smoked bacon lardons and cook until brown and crispy.

12. Add the peppers and fennel to the lardons. Turn down the heat and cook gently until the vegetables are soft but not coloured. Add the cooking liquor from the mussels and the aubergine pulp, and stir to combine.

13. Add the mussels and cook until steaming hot.

14. Turn into a large bowl, scatter over the basil leaves and serve immediately.

In place of the star anise, try a little Pernod, to taste, instead.

Salmon en Croûte

Try to get wild salmon, even though this is a little more expensive, or use a good-quality Scottish farmed salmon. Pernod gives it a hint of aniseed flavour.

SERVES: 4–6
PREPARATION TIME: 20–25 MINUTES
COOKING TIME: 30–40 MINUTES

sea salt and freshly ground black pepper
300g raw king prawns, peeled and thawed
   if frozen
600g salmon fillet, skinned and boned
3–4 tablespoons olive oil
3–4 whole sprigs fresh thyme
3–4 leaves fresh basil
3 tablespoons pastis or Pernod (optional)
1 lemon (see method)
1 garlic clove, peeled
300g baby leaf spinach, washed and well
   drained
300g all-butter ready-made puff pastry
2 x 20cm cooked pancakes (see page 216)
3 medium eggs, hard-boiled, shelled and
   halved lengthways
25g Cheddar cheese, thinly sliced
2–3 tablespoons capers, well drained

Mornay sauce
20g butter, diced
20g plain flour
200–250ml milk, warmed
100g Brie (or similar cheese),
   broken into pieces
Egg wash
1–2 medium egg yolks
1 teaspoon cold water
pinch salt

When making the sauce, it is important to use equal quantities of butter and flour. Also, always warm the milk first. Cooking the spinach quickly retains its colour, vitamins and nutrients.

1. Season the prawns and salmon well. Line a baking tray with baking parchment.

2. Heat a heavy-based frying pan with 1 tablespoon oil. Quickly fry the salmon on both sides, together with half the thyme and basil, until pale golden brown, roughly 2 minutes. Do not overcook it.

3. Sprinkle over the pastis or Pernod (if using). With the lemon under the palm of your hand, roll it hard over the work surface to release the juices. Cut it in half and squeeze both halves over the fish. Lift out the salmon carefully and lay on a plate. Set aside.

4. In the same pan, fry the prawns until pink and set aside. Again, do not overcook them.

5. Rub the garlic around the pan used for cooking the salmon and prawns. Add the spinach and a splash of cold water. Cover with a lid and cook for 5–10 seconds or until wilted. Remove the spinach and carefully squeeze dry. Set aside.

6. Again using the same pan, make the sauce by melting the butter. Tip in the flour and stir well for 1–2 minutes to ensure that the flour is cooked. Add the milk gradually, stirring constantly. When fully amalgamated, stir in the cheese and remove immediately from the heat to allow it to melt. Season to taste.

7. Preheat the oven to 180°C/Fan 160°C/Gas 4. Make the egg wash by beating together the egg yolks with the water and salt.

8. Roll out the pastry to form a rectangle about 30cm long and 15cm wide. Place one pancake in the centre of the pastry and top with the whole cooked salmon. Spoon over half of the cheese sauce, top with the prawns, then the spinach. Carefully lay the eggs on top, yolk side down, then cover with the remaining cheese sauce, followed by the Cheddar cheese.

9. Carefully spoon the capers over the top. Finally add the remaining herbs and the last pancake. Press down firmly to compress all the layers.

10. Bring up the two long sides of pastry, brush the edges with egg wash and crimp together well. Fold the two ends of pastry up over the middle seam and seal well. Lay carefully on the prepared baking tray with the seam on the underside. Brush well with egg wash. Snip the edges with a pair of scissors to create a pattern, making sure not to pierce the pastry.

11. Bake in the preheated oven for 30–45 minutes or until well risen and golden brown.

12. Serve hot with new season boiled potatoes and seasonal vegetables.

Baked Aubergines with Baby Vegetables

Aubergines are one of my favourite vegetables, and this is guaranteed to be a great dish.

SERVES: 2
PREPARATION TIME: 35 MINUTES
COOKING TIME: 10 MINUTES
MARINATING TIME: 2–3 HOURS

2 medium aubergines, halved lengthways
1 tablespoon caster sugar
1 teaspoon salt
150ml olive oil
1–2 garlic cloves, peeled and chopped
3–4 whole sprigs fresh lemon thyme
2 tablespoons runny honey
150–175g mixed baby vegetables, prepared
   (mangetout, baby leeks, button
   mushrooms, asparagus tips, courgettes,
   baby fennel, ripe cherry vine tomatoes)
2–3 leaves fresh basil, torn
freshly ground black pepper
2 large red peppers, stalks removed,
   deseeded and chopped
1–2 teaspoons lemon juice
caster sugar
4 tablespoons black olive tapenade
100g medium-soft cheese (e.g. Toppenrose
   or Brie), sliced

1. Place the aubergine halves in a non-metallic dish and sprinkle the cut surfaces with the sugar and salt. Leave for 2–3 hours, loosely covered, in the fridge.

2. Preheat the oven to 200°C/Fan 180°C/Gas 6.

3. Remove the aubergine halves with a slotted spoon and reserve the juices. Heat an ovenproof frying pan until hot with 75ml of the oil. Fry the aubergine halves for 2–3 minutes on both sides until golden brown.

4. Add the garlic, lemon thyme and drizzle over the honey, shaking the pan from time to time to prevent sticking. Cook for a couple of minutes and then pour over the reserved aubergine juices and bake in the preheated oven for 15 minutes.

5. Meanwhile, heat a frying pan with 45ml of the oil and when hot, sauté the baby vegetables (with the exception of the tomatoes) until al dente – this should take 2–3 minutes. Season to taste and add 2 tablespoons water. Cover with a lid and cook for about 2 minutes or until all the water has evaporated. Add the tomatoes, together with the basil.

6. Next, process or juice the red peppers, and cook the pulp in a small pan until reduced by half. Add lemon juice and sugar to taste. This should yield 4–6 tablespoons pepper juice.

7. To assemble, top the aubergine halves with the baby vegetables. Spoon the tapenade evenly over and top with the slices of cheese. Drizzle over the pepper juice and the remaining oil, and return to the hot oven for a further 15–20 minutes.

8. Serve garnished with some more lemon thyme and with the juices from the pan drizzled over.

Merlot-braised Oxtail with Pan-fried Ricotta Gnocchi

Oxtail requires long, slow cooking but it is certainly worth the wait. Most supermarkets and butchers sell oxtail during the winter months as it is regarded as a comfort food. I serve this recipe with freshly made ricotta gnocchi...delicious!

SERVES: 4
PREPARATION TIME: 30 MINUTES
COOKING TIME: 3–4 HOURS
INFUSION TIME: 1 HOUR

50ml vegetable oil
1kg oxtail, trimmed
salt and freshly ground black pepper
5 shallots, peeled and finely sliced
2 carrots, peeled and diced
4 whole sprigs fresh thyme
1 bay leaf
plain flour for sprinkling
1 litre Merlot (or similar red wine)
350ml ruby port

pinch caster sugar
1 tablespoon tomato purée
200g tomatoes, chopped
500ml hot chicken stock
4 garlic cloves, halved, core removed and crushed
1 quantity ricotta gnocchi (see page 202)
To serve
Parmesan shavings

1. Heat half the oil in a heavy-based ovenproof pan and add the oxtail. Season well. Allow to brown on all sides, then add the shallots, carrots, thyme and bay leaf. Cook until the vegetables are just soft and slightly coloured. Sprinkle over some flour.

2. Pour in the wine and port, and stir in the sugar. Bring to the boil, skimming off any impurities with a small ladle or spoon. Then reduce the heat and simmer for 45 minutes, uncovered, or until the liquid is reduced by half.

3. Preheat the oven to 140°C/Fan 120°C/Gas 1. Add the tomato purée and tomatoes, and pour in the stock. Bring to the boil, cover with the lid and cook in the preheated oven for 3–4 hours or until cooked and tender, checking every hour that it has not dried out.

4. Remove from the oven and add the garlic. Leave covered and undisturbed at room temperature to infuse for 1 hour.

5. Remove the oxtail with a slotted spoon, reserving the cooking liquor. Cut the meat off the bone and set aside to keep warm.

6. Reduce the cooking liquor until it is the consistency of a sauce, roughly 20–30 minutes.

7. Meanwhile, heat a non-stick pan with the remaining olive oil. When hot, dust the gnocchi with a little flour and fry until slightly coloured.

8. When the sauce is the correct consistency, add the oxtail and heat gently, stirring well to combine. Season to taste.

9. To serve, ladle out the sauce on to hot plates, followed by the gnocchi and sprinkled with Parmesan shavings.

This recipe is equally good with lamb or pork shank. Simply adjust the cooking time accordingly. Add just enough flour to soak up the fat.

The Best Beef and Cheese Lasagne

The blend of minced beef and Camembert cheese is a wonderful combination and is complemented by a good red wine. I try to use organic meat whenever I can and always look out for low-fat versions. I fell so in love with this recipe that I introduced it to Geir Frantzen, the owner of Findus, and Vidar Engen, his manager director, and it was immediately chosen to be the first dish from my Novelli/Findus frozen ready-meal range. Already a best seller!

SERVES: 4
PREPARATION TIME: 45 MINUTES
COOKING TIME: 50–60 MINUTES

Tomato sauce
4 tablespoons olive oil
1 x 400g can chopped tomatoes
1 garlic clove, peeled and crushed
pinch caster sugar
1 sprig fresh thyme, stalks removed
   and chopped
1 bay leaf
1 vanilla pod, halved lengthways
1 star anise
sea salt and freshly ground pepper
Meat sauce
3 tablespoons olive oil
1 onion or 4 shallots, peeled and
   finely diced
400g lean minced beef
1 sprig fresh thyme, stalks removed

2 bay leaves
2 fresh basil leaves, torn
375ml Italian red wine (e.g. Chianti
   or Merlot)
pinch caster sugar
2 teaspoons tomato purée
Camembert sauce
20g unsalted butter
20g plain flour
60ml hot vegetable or beef stock
100ml double cream
250g mature Camembert cheese
freshly grated nutmeg (to taste)

4 sheets of fresh white lasagne
1 garlic clove, peeled and halved

1. First, make the tomato sauce. Heat the oil in a heavy-based pan and add the tomatoes and garlic. When the tomatoes start to release their juices add the sugar, herbs, spices and seasoning. Cook over a gentle heat for 10 minutes or until the tomatoes are reduced and thick.

2. Meanwhile, make the meat sauce. Heat the oil in a separate heavy-based frying pan. Sauté the onion or shallots for 3–5 minutes or until soft but not coloured.

3. Add the beef and cook for 5–8 minutes or until the meat is browned. Add the herbs, and pour in the wine. Reduce slowly over a gentle heat until thick. Do not allow to boil so that the meat can fully absorb the flavour of the wine.

4. Skim the meat sauce if necessary. Season to taste, and add sugar to taste. Stir in the tomato purée and take out the bay leaves.

5. To make the Camembert sauce, melt the butter in a saucepan and add the flour. Stir for 1–2 minutes, making sure that the flour is cooked but does not brown.

6. Pour in the hot stock slowly, stirring all the time to prevent lumps forming. When fully incorporated, stir in the cream.

7. With a vegetable peeler, shave off most off the Camembert skin and discard. Break the cheese into small pieces and add to the sauce, stirring well until melted. Season to taste and add the nutmeg.

8. Remove the bay leaf, vanilla and star anise from the tomato sauce and combine this with the meat sauce and three quarters of the Camembert sauce.

9. Bring a pan of salted water to the boil and add 2–3 drops olive oil. When boiling, blanch the lasagne sheets for 4–5 minutes. Remove and drain.

10. To assemble the lasagne, rub the halved garlic around the inside of a lightly greased ovenproof dish, 24cm x 15cm. Preheat the oven to 160°C/Fan 140°C/Gas 3.

11. Put one sheet of pasta in the base of the prepared dish, top with one third of the meat sauce, then add another sheet of pasta. Cover with one third of the meat sauce, then another sheet of pasta, followed by the remainder of the meat sauce and the final sheet of pasta.

12. Spoon over the remaining cheese sauce. Cook in the preheated oven for 30–40 minutes or until golden brown and cooked through. Serve with a watercress, avocado and toasted pine nut salad.

To make it easier to remove the skin, put the Camembert in the freezer for 5 minutes before peeling. A pinch of sugar brings out the sweetness of the tomatoes.

Slow Braised Honey and Cider Caramelised Pork Belly

This recipe melts in your mouth. It is made from a mixture of herbs and spices and flavoured with a good quality cider, which gives it a lovely apple taste. Serve this with caramelised onion mashed potato.

SERVES: 4
PREPARATION TIME: 25 MINUTES
COOKING TIME: 1½ HOURS

2 large white onions, peeled, halved and sliced
1.5kg pork belly, with rind removed but the fat left on (ask your local or supermarket butcher to prepare)
sea salt and freshly ground black pepper
1 quantity olive oil mash (see page 195)

Braising liquor
1 litre good-quality dry cider (do not use sweet cider)
150ml runny honey
1 beef stock cube
1 star anise
1 teaspoon fennel seeds
4 whole sprigs fresh thyme
sea salt

1. In a frying pan, dry-fry the onions until caramelised.

2. Heat an ovenproof cast-iron pan. Season the pork belly and dry-fry on both sides, fat side first, until golden brown, ensuring that all sides of the meat are sealed. Remove from the pan and set aside to rest for 3–5 minutes. (Most of the fat should have been released during this stage.)

3. Preheat the oven to 180°C/Fan 160°C/Gas 4. Transfer the pork to a baking tray and cover with cling film. Place a heavy chopping board on top and press down hard. (This allows for a neater presentation when it is cooked.)

4. Remove the cling film. Lay the onions on the pork fat residue in the ovenproof pan and cover with the pork belly.

5. In a bowl, combine all the ingredients for the braising liquor. Pour over the pork belly and cook in the preheated oven for 1½ hours.

6. Remove from the oven, lift the meat out of the pan to rest for 10 minutes and set aside. With a slotted spoon, remove the onions and add to the olive oil mash (see page 195). Reduce the remaining liquor to the consistency of a sauce.

7. Serve the pork hot with the olive oil mash and sauce.

Instead of onions you can use large shallots or fennel.

Maman Novelli Chicken Fricassee

This is one of my mother's favourite recipes that she has handed down to me. I remember she always said to use the best ingredients that you can afford and you can't go wrong. It's even better reheated the next day.

SERVES: 4
PREPARATION TIME: 25 MINUTES
COOKING TIME: 45 MINUTES

salt and freshly ground black pepper
4 chicken portions, halved or quartered, depending on size
50ml extra-virgin olive oil
1 white onion, peeled and sliced
1 bay leaf
1 sprig fresh thyme, stalk removed
1 teaspoon cumin seeds
1 teaspoon plain flour

600ml dry white wine
1 chicken stock cube
300g long-grain white rice
200ml double cream
150g good-quality stoned olives, black or green
1 tablespoon flat-leaf parsley, chopped
pinch freshly grated nutmeg

1. Preheat the oven to 180°C/Fan 160°C/Gas 4.

2. Season the chicken pieces. Heat half the oil in a large deep ovenproof pan with a lid and colour the chicken on both sides. Remove and place in a bowl to keep warm.

3. Drizzle the remaining oil into the pan and sweat the onion gently until softened. Add the bay leaf, thyme and cumin, then return the chicken to the pan. Sift over the flour and allow to cook out, for 1–2 minutes, so that it absorbs the fat completely.

4. Pour in the wine and crumble in the stock cube. Add the rice and bring to the boil. Once at boiling point, cover the pan with the lid and put in the preheated oven for 45 minutes.

5. Remove from the oven. On a low heat on the hob, stir in the cream, olives, parsley and nutmeg. Heat through before serving.

When adding the flour to the chicken, use only enough for the fat to be absorbed. For the best flavour choose an organic or corn-fed chicken.

Hot Apricot Flan

This dessert can be made all year round using canned fruit but when apricots are in season, halve, stone and cook them in the microwave for a few minutes first (covered in a little water). Serve hot or cold in wedges.

SERVES: 4–6
PREPARATION TIME: 30–35 MINUTES, PLUS 1 HOUR MARINATING
CHILLING TIME: 45 MINUTES
COOKING TIME: 15–20 MINUTES
COOLING TIME: 15–20 MINUTES

200–250g canned apricot halves
50ml kirsch
30ml runny honey
vegetable or light olive oil
Filling
pinch salt
150g demerara sugar
the seeds from 1 vanilla pod
100ml runny honey

20g salted butter, softened
4 medium eggs
250g plain flour, sifted
600ml milk
400ml double cream
For coating
10g caster sugar
10g cocoa powder

1. Drain the apricots, discarding the juice, and turn into a bowl. Add the kirsch and allow to macerate for 1 hour.

2. Preheat the oven to 180°C/Fan 160°C/Gas 4. Grease a 22cm deep-sided flan tin with butter and chill in the fridge for 5 minutes.

3. Meanwhile, make the filling. In a bowl, beat together the salt, demerara sugar, vanilla, honey, butter and eggs. Gradually sift the flour into the bowl, beating well to prevent lumps forming. Add the milk and cream, beating well. Cover and leave in the fridge to rest for 20 minutes.

4. In the meantime, remove the flan tin from the fridge and grease with a little more butter. Sift the sugar and cocoa powder together and use to dust the tin, shaking it to ensure even distribution over the butter. Return to the fridge for another 20 minutes.

5. Remove the tin from the fridge and spoon in the prepared filling.

6. Add the 30ml honey to the apricots. This coats the fruit and helps to prevent it from sinking. Arrange the apricots on top of the filling and brush them with a little oil.

7. Bake in the preheated oven for 15–20 minutes or until golden brown and cooked through.

8. Allow to cool for 15–20 minutes before serving in wedges with scoops of vanilla ice-cream or crème fraîche.

White Chocolate and Passion Fruit Toffee Cup

Passion fruit and white chocolate are a delicious combination, and they are even better when served, as here, with toffee and a hint of whisky and kirsch. This recipe can be made in advance and should be served well chilled.

SERVES: 2–3
PREPARATION TIME: 20 MINUTES
CHILLING TIME: 2 HOURS MINIMUM
COOKING TIME: 20–25 MINUTES

300g white chocolate, broken in pieces
4 passion fruit, flesh only
300ml double cream, chilled
75ml kirsch
80ml crème fraîche
15g flaked almonds, toasted

Toffee
200g soft brown sugar
200ml double cream
25–30ml whisky

1. Melt the white chocolate in a bain-marie or a bowl set over a pan of simmering water. Ensure that the bottom of the bowl does not touch the water.

2. When the chocolate has melted, stir in the flesh from the passion fruit. Whisk in the cream and the kirsch, and set aside.

3. Make the toffee. Turn the sugar into a heavy-based saucepan. Cover with water and heat gently until the sugar has melted. When it starts to turn into caramel, pour in the double cream, stirring all the time. Add the whisky and continue to cook. After about 10 minutes when it has reached toffee consistency, set it aside.

4. Have 2–3 cups, depending on their size, ready for serving. Layer the mixtures, starting with the white chocolate at the bottom, followed by the toffee and the crème fraîche.

5. Leave to set in the fridge for at least 2 hours.

6. When ready to serve, scatter over the flaked almonds.

These can be made up to 3 days in advance. Mango can be used instead of passion fruit.

Choco Pot Kahlúa

This is a pudding with a great blend of flavours – chocolate and coffee. It will only take one mouthful for it to melt in your mouth and win you compliments every time. You will need 6 ceramic pots or coffee cups for this recipe, 175ml capacity.

SERVES: 6
PREPARATION TIME: 10–15 MINUTES
CHILLING TIME: 12 HOURS
COOKING TIME: 20 MINUTES

2 medium egg yolks
30ml runny honey
50ml Kahlúa
100ml milk
100ml single cream
400ml double cream
400g bitter chocolate, 70 per cent cocoa
   solids, broken in pieces

To serve
50g icing sugar, sifted
the seeds from ¼ vanilla pod
150–200ml whipping cream
cocoa powder, sifted

1. Combine the egg yolks, honey and Kahlúa in a bowl.

2. In a saucepan, bring the milk and creams to the boil. Add the broken chocolate into the cream, stirring until it melts on a very low heat.

3. Remove from the heat and stir into the egg yolks, honey and Kahlúa.

4. Divide between 6 ceramic pots or coffee cups (each holding roughly 175ml) and chill in the fridge for at least 12 hours before serving.

5. When ready to serve, add the sugar and vanilla to the cream and whip until it thickens slightly. Spoon a dollop of cream on to each pot and dust with the sifted cocoa powder to create a cappuccino effect.

Kirsch, Mango and Pomegranate Rice Pudding

Pomegranates are one of the super foods and they are now available all year round. Some supermarkets even sell them already prepared in the chiller section. They contain more vitamin C than any other fruit.

SERVES: 6–8
PREPARATION TIME: 20 MINUTES
COOKING TIME: 50 MINUTES

Syrup
25g caster sugar
50ml water
Rice pudding
500g arborio or carnaroli risotto rice
2 vanilla pods, halved lengthways
30g desiccated coconut
750ml milk
50g caster sugar
White chocolate cream
200g white chocolate, broken in pieces
175ml double cream
50ml mango purée (see tip below)

Pomegranate syrup
200ml pomegranate pulp, deseeded
1½ vanilla pods, halved lengthways
    and deseeded
80g demerara sugar
50ml kirsch
juice of 1 lemon
To serve
250–300g crème fraîche
cocoa powder to sprinkle

1. First, make the syrup. Dissolve the sugar in the water in a medium saucepan on a low heat and, when dissolved, simmer for 3–4 minutes. Remove from the heat.

2. Whilst the syrup is still hot, add the rice, vanilla pods and desiccated coconut.

3. In a separate pan, heat the milk and sugar until tepid and then add to the rice. Cook over a moderate heat, stirring constantly, until all the milk has been absorbed, and the rice is soft and creamy, which will take about 35–40 minutes. If necessary, add more milk to prevent the rice from drying out. Remove from the heat and set aside to cool before removing the vanilla pods.

4. Next, make the cream. Melt the chocolate in a bain-marie or a bowl set over a pan of simmering water, making sure that the water does not touch the base of the bowl. When fully melted, remove from the heat and leave to cool. When cooled, stir in the cream and mango purée.

5. Finally, make the pomegranate syrup. Turn the pomegranate pulp and vanilla into a pan and allow to sweat over a low heat for 2–3 minutes.

6. Add the sugar, reduce the heat further and cook gently for 5 minutes. Remove from the heat and stir in the kirsch and lemon juice.

7. To serve, place a layer of rice pudding into the bottom of each individual glass dish. Add a layer, half as deep, of crème fraîche. Follow this with a layer of pomegranate and another, half as deep again, of crème fraîche. Finish with a layer of white chocolate cream, another layer of crème fraîche and a sprinkle of cocoa powder.

This dessert is perfect for dinner parties because it can be made up to 3 days in advance. To make the mango purée, liquidise 50g of the fruit with a splash of water to loosen it and strain through a sieve.

DINNER PARTY

Hannes's Amazing 'Bad Gastein' Radish Soup

Chilled Beetroot Gazpacho

Roasted Vine Tomato Tarts with Rocket
  Crème Fraîche

Prawn and Salmon Soufflé with Roquefort

Bamboo-steamed Monkfish Osso-Bucco Style

Roast Loin of Pork with Armagnac and
  Prune Stuffing

Baked Cod Dauphinois

Roast Chicken Crown with Sweet Lemon
  and Thyme

Oven-glazed Beef Fillet 'Mich Mich'

Oven-roasted Lamb Cutlets Glazed
  with Roquefort

Iced Raspberry Soufflés with Vanilla
  and Yogurt

Baked Apple Soufflés with Chocolate and
  Kirsch Sauce

Rich Dark and White Chocolate Fondants

Whole Baked Oranges with Crème Brûlée

Caramelised Pear and Cranberry Tarte Tatin

Hannes's Amazing 'Bad Gastein' Radish Soup

While on holiday in the most beautiful part of Austria, I came across this fantastic recipe which never fails to please. Try it for yourself and I am sure you will agree it is one of the best soups in the world! It is produced by one of the many great chefs of Austria, where in every restaurant, in general, you can discover the most consistent, professional and impeccable service.

SERVES: 4–6
PREPARATION TIME: 10 MINUTES
COOKING TIME: 20 MINUTES

50g butter
300g radishes, trimmed and thinly sliced
1 tablespoon plain flour
1 teaspoon tomato purée
1 litre hot beef stock

500ml double cream
salt and freshly ground black pepper
Garnish
double cream
3 radishes, cut into fine strips

1. Melt the butter in a saucepan, add the radishes and cook gently for 2 minutes.

2. Sprinkle in the flour, stir in the tomato purée and pour in the hot stock. Stir to combine and cook at a simmer for 15 minutes or until the radishes are tender.

3. Remove from the heat and blitz in a blender or food processor, adding the cream. Season to taste.

4. Return to a clean pan to reheat and serve hot, garnished with a dollop of double cream and a few radish strips.

To give this recipe a different twist, when you are reheating, add 1 tablespoon of vinegar or lemon juice, to taste. Because the stock is hot when it is added, the cooking time is reduced, which means more flavour and more nutrients.

Chilled Beetroot Gazpacho

Choose young and tender beetroot for this recipe. I like to grow my own, but it is up to you. Occasionally I add a touch of sugar. This is such a quick recipe to make, especially on a hot summer's day. The secret to my recipe is to chill everything before serving.

SERVES: 3–4
PREPARATION TIME: 5 MINUTES
CHILLING TIME: 2–3 HOURS

450g overripe tomatoes
2 shallots, peeled
1 overripe red pepper, stalk removed
  and deseeded
1 garlic clove, peeled
½ cucumber
150g cooked beetroot (vacuum packed,
  juice included)

150–200ml olive oil
20ml sherry vinegar
1 red chilli, finely chopped
½–1 tablespoon caster sugar
salt and freshly ground black pepper
50ml water

1. Put the tomatoes, shallots, red pepper, garlic, cucumber and beetroot (plus its juice), together with the olive oil, into a blender or food processor and blitz until smooth.

2. Add the sherry vinegar, chilli and sugar, and season to taste. If too thick, add a little water.

3. Decant into a glass container and chill in the fridge for 2–3 hours.

4. Serve chilled.

Use a glass container to chill the soup because glass is an excellent conductor of cold. All the ingredients for this recipe should be at room temperature before use.

Roasted Vine Tomato Tarts with Rocket Crème Fraîche

For this recipe, the tomatoes have to be baked twice. This may seem a long drawn out process, but the end result is well worth it. For the best flavour, ovenbake the tomatoes for the first time on the day before you need them, although you can still make the dish with a great result on the same day. This is a dish that my friends Neil and Tracy Wager manage to produce perfectly when we go to stay with them. You will either need 9cm blinis pans, as here, or you can make this as one large tart.

SERVES: 4
PREPARATION TIME: 15 MINUTES
COOKING TIME: 4 HOURS

16 Roma (fresh plum) tomatoes
12 fresh basil leaves
8 tablespoons basil oil (see page 232 and make this oil using only basil leaves)
3 tablespoons balsamic syrup, store-bought or see tip overleaf
25g caster sugar
25g coarse sea salt
25g freshly ground black pepper
150g wild rocket
100ml crème fraîche
½ vanilla pod, halved lengthways
500g ready-made puff pastry
50g unsalted butter
100g Parmesan, finely grated
juice of ½ lemon

1. Preheat the oven to 130°C/Fan 110°C/Gas ½. Line a baking sheet with baking parchment.

2. Wash the tomatoes well, remove the stalks and cut in half vertically through the centre. Place on the prepared baking sheet, cut side facing upwards.

3. Roll up 8 basil leaves and cut into fine strips. Scatter evenly over the tomatoes.

4. Sprinkle the tomatoes evenly with 1 tablespoon basil oil, 1 tablespoon balsamic syrup and half the caster sugar, sea salt and freshly ground black pepper. Bake in the preheated oven for 3 hours. Remove them from the oven, cover and set aside in a dry place (not the fridge) until required.

5. For the rocket crème fraîche, blanch 20g of the rocket leaves in boiling water for 3 seconds. Squeeze out the excess water and, while still hot, blitz in a blender or food processor with half the crème fraîche, blending until smooth. Cover and chill in the fridge.

6. Choose the best 16 tomato halves for the tart and gently reshape if necessary. Dry them well with kitchen paper and place on a clean baking tray. Set aside.

7. Turn the remaining tomatoes, together with the cooking liquor, into a small saucepan. Add the vanilla pod and 3 tablespoons basil oil. Allow to reduce very slowly on a low heat for 25 minutes. Remove and discard the vanilla pod, and push the tomato pulp through a fine sieve. Chill in the fridge until needed. *Recipe continued overleaf*

8. Roll out the puff pastry to a 5mm thickness and cut out 4 discs, each 9cm in diameter. Chill in the fridge until needed.

9. Set a heavy-based frying pan over a low heat and add 3 teaspoons basil oil.

10. Sprinkle the reserved tomato halves with 1 tablespoon basil oil, 1 tablespoon balsamic syrup and the remaining caster sugar, sea salt and freshly ground black pepper.

11. Gently fry in the preheated pan, cut side down, until starting to colour, about 2–3 minutes. Add the butter and remove from the heat. Allow to cool.

12. Preheat the oven to 180°C/Fan 160°C/Gas 4.

13. Place the twice-cooked tomatoes, face down, in the blinis pans, 4 to each pan: 1 in the centre with the other 3 tucked around it. Remove the tomato sauce from the fridge and spoon 1 tablespoon over the centre of each of the tomatoes, reserving the remaining sauce, and lay a single basil leaf over the central tomato in each pan. Cover with a disc of pastry, making sure to crimp in the sides.

14. Place in the preheated oven and bake for 15 minutes.

15. Reduce the heat to 160°C/Fan 140°C/Gas 3 and bake for a further 15 minutes. Remove and set aside but do not allow to cool completely.

16. Meanwhile, wash the remaining rocket leaves in ice-cold water and drain well, making sure that all excess water has been removed. Turn into a bowl.

17. Put half the grated Parmesan into a small saucepan with the remaining crème fraîche. Warm gently until the cheese has melted.

18. Add the remaining Parmesan to the rocket, together with the lemon juice, and the remaining basil oil and balsamic syrup. Season to taste and toss thoroughly with your hands.

19. To serve, gently turn over the tarts while they are still warm and place them, pastry side down, on to serving plates. Spoon a little of the remaining tomato sauce over the top and spread evenly. Place a spoonful of the rocket crème fraiche on top, so that it starts to melt, and place a portion of the rocket salad alongside. Finally, drizzle with the warm Parmesan sauce.

Take 6 tablespoons of balsamic vinegar and 2 tablespoons of honey; reduce down until you are left with about 3 tablespoons for the recipe.

Prawn and Salmon Soufflé with Roquefort

This recipe can be made with scallops, chicken, lobster, sole, and so on, in place of the prawns and salmon. Just make sure the eggs are at room temperature and are very fresh.

SERVES: 6
PREPARATION TIME: 15–20 MINUTES
CHILLING TIME: 1 HOUR
COOKING TIME: 8–10 MINUTES

butter, for greasing
250g raw tiger prawns
250g raw salmon
salt and freshly ground black pepper
3 medium egg whites
400ml double cream

225ml whipping cream, whisked
  to light peaks
1 large courgette
olive oil
35g Roquefort, cut into 6 cubes

1. Preheat the oven to 200°C/Fan 180°C/Gas 4. Grease 6 small ramekins with butter.

2. In a blender or food processor, blitz the prawns and salmon together. Season to taste. With the motor running, add the eggs one at a time, ensuring each is incorporated before adding the next.

3. Again with the motor still running, pour in the double cream through the funnel. Do not overprocess at this stage. Do it just enough to ensure that it is fully incorporated.

4. Turn into a glass bowl and, using a spatula, carefully fold in the whipping cream. Cover and chill in the fridge until needed but for at least an hour.

5. Slice the courgette lengthways, using a mandolin, or very thinly, using a knife.

6. Dip each slice into the olive oil, coating both sides, and then arrange around the inside of the buttered ramekins.

7. Remove the fish paste from the fridge and divide between the ramekins. Top each with a cube of Roquefort.

8. Bake in the preheated oven for 8–10 minutes until risen and golden brown. Serve immediately.

For a bit of variety add ½ teaspoon of paprika or place a fresh basil leaf under each piece of cheese before baking.

Bamboo-steamed Monkfish Osso-Bucco Style

Make sure the monkfish pieces are not too large otherwise you will lose tenderness in the fish. And, whatever you do, use top quality ingredients and be sure to remove the thick skin. You will need a steamer and a large freezer or sandwich bag for this recipe.

SERVES: 8
PREPARATION TIME: 30 MINUTES
CHILLING TIME: 24 HOURS
COOKING TIME: 25 MINUTES

8 x 80g monkfish fillets, tail pieces
8 fresh basil leaves
8 baby carrots, blanched, peeled and
    trimmed into 6cm pieces, retaining
    the thicker end
50ml olive oil, plus extra for drizzling
1 bay leaf
6 sprigs fresh thyme, stalks removed
1 garlic clove, peeled and finely chopped
juice of ½ lemon
sprinkle of fennel seeds
1 star anise
salt and freshly ground black pepper
800g baby spinach

4 sprigs fresh chervil
salt and freshly ground black pepper
Sauce
10ml olive oil
2 banana shallots, peeled and sliced
1 bay leaf
3 sprigs fresh thyme, stalks removed
750ml red wine (e.g. Barolo or Merlot)
2 black peppercorns
50g caster sugar *or* 50ml runny honey
50ml double cream
80–100g unsalted butter, diced
1 garlic clove, peeled, halved and
    core removed

1. Lay the monkfish on a flat surface and make a small hole through the middle of each piece.

2. Wrap a basil leaf tightly around each carrot and push through the hole. Repeat with the remaining fish pieces. Put the fish into the freezer or sandwich bag.

3. In a bowl, combine the olive oil, bay leaf, thyme, garlic, lemon juice, fennel seeds and star anise. Pour into the bag and shake gently to coat the fish. Squeeze out the air, seal the bag and refrigerate for 24 hours.

4. Make the sauce. Heat a saucepan, add the olive oil and shallots, and cook for 1 minute. Add the bay leaf, thyme, red wine, peppercorns and sugar or honey. Stir until the sugar is dissolved.

5. Reduce the wine until a light syrup is achieved. Stir in the cream and bring to the boil. Sieve this into another saucepan. *Recipe continued overleaf*

6. Remove from the heat. Whisk in the butter and then add the garlic. Set aside to cool until required.

7. Heat a steamer. When the water is boiling, remove the fish from the bag with a slotted spoon (but do not discard the bag). Season and place carefully into the hot steamer. Steam for 4–6 minutes.

8. Meanwhile, place the spinach in the freezer bag, add seasoning to taste and shake gently to coat the leaves with the marinade.

9. When the fish is cooked, remove from the steamer and set aside in a warm place to rest. Keep the steamer on the boil.

10. In a separate saucepan, heat the sauce, but do not allow it to boil.

11. Remove the spinach from the bag and place it in the steamer. Steam for 1 minute.

12. To serve, pour a little sauce on to each serving plate. Add a portion of spinach topped by two pieces of fish. To finish, drizzle with a little olive oil and garnish with the chervil.

Alternatively, leave the fish whole but cut it into 4 and wrap each piece in Parma ham. Steam it for 6 minutes, then pan-fry and serve in the same way. You could also use thinly sliced smoked pork belly instead of Parma ham. *Make sure you use a bamboo steamer.*

Roast Loin of Pork with Armagnac and Prune Stuffing

An alternative Sunday roast, this reminds me of working alongside the very talented young British chefs, Phil Thomson and Martin Thousand, who have always impressed me with their versatile way of cooking. Phil would adapt this and use dates, apricots, raisins, dried peach or dried pineapple instead of prunes.

SERVES: 6
PREPARATION TIME: 1 HOUR
COOKING TIME: 1 HOUR 45 MINUTES

1.75kg boned loin of pork, skin scored
3 tablespoons olive oil
1 garlic clove, crushed
sea salt

Prune and armagnac stuffing
300g prunes
300ml good-quality armagnac
salt and freshly ground black pepper
1 heaped tablespoon fresh sage, chopped

1. Preheat the oven to 220°C/Fan 200°C/Gas 7.

2. To make the stuffing, soak the prunes in the armagnac for 30 minutes.

3. Remove with a slotted spoon and drain, reserving the armagnac. Season to taste. Over a low heat, gently sauté the prunes in a drizzle of olive oil until they begin to collapse. Pour over the armagnac and flambé, remove from the heat and add the sage. Allow to cool.

4. With a long, thin, sharp knife, cut the fat away from the pork loin on three of the four sides. Layer the prunes on top of the meat and then fold the fat back over the top.

5. Heat the oil in a pan, add the garlic and allow it to infuse for one minute.

6. Put the joint fat-side down in a roasting tin on a trivet. Pour over the hot oil and sprinkle liberally with sea salt. Roast in the preheated oven for about 3/4 hour, turn the meat over so that fat is now on top and return to the oven. Cook for a further 3/4 hour, or until the juices run clear.

7. If the crackling is not quite crisp, remove and return to the oven. Meanwhile, transfer the pork to a dish and allow it to rest for 10 minutes covered with foil.

Make sure you use organic pork. Remove the rind and start cooking the pork fat side down.

Baked Cod Dauphinois

Using turbot would create a more prestigious result, but it is more expensive and a little bit more technique is required, though it would be worth it, especially for a dinner party. The gratin dauphinois for this recipe can be made 24 hours in advance (see page 191).

SERVES: 4
PREPARATION TIME: 10–15 MINUTES
COOKING TIME: 20–25 MINUTES

1 quantity gratin dauphinois (see page 191)
12 fresh basil leaves
4 x 150g thick cod fillets
8 slices Swiss cheese (Gruyère or Emmenthal)

4 bay leaves
70g caul fat (available from your butcher)
salt and freshly ground black pepper
10ml olive oil

1. Preheat the oven to 180°C/Fan 160°C/Gas 4.

2. Using a 6cm diameter cutter, divide the gratin dauphinois into 4 portions. Place 3 basil leaves on top of each cod fillet.

3. Lay 1 slice of cheese over each portion of fish, followed by the dauphinois. Lightly press down so that the potato covers the fish evenly. Add the remaining slices of cheese and top each portion with 1 bay leaf.

4. Open out the caul fat and use it to cover each fish portion, creating a tight even parcel. Pat dry with kitchen paper to remove any excess moisture and season to taste.

5. Heat the olive oil in a heavy-based ovenproof pan. Add the fish and bake in the preheated oven for 20–25 minutes or until golden brown.

Alternatively, steam the fish for 15 minutes, then lay on buttered foil before baking in the preheated oven for 10 minutes. If the top of the cod dauphinois has not coloured then you can flash it under a preheated grill.

Roast Chicken Crown with Sweet Lemon and Thyme

This is an original way to cook roast chicken. You will need to cook the legs longer than the breast, therefore, make sure you slice and detach the legs from the crown. You can use either stock alone or a mixture of half stock and half wine for the accompanying risotto.

SERVES: 2
PREPARATION TIME: 25–30 MINUTES
COOKING TIME: 60 MINUTES

Squash
1 butternut squash, weighing approx.
   300–400g
3 teaspoons olive oil
sea salt and freshly ground black pepper
3–4 sprigs fresh rosemary
3 sprigs fresh thyme
1 whole garlic bulb, unpeeled, halved
   horizontally
Chicken
1 lemon
3–4 tablespoons runny honey
3 sprigs fresh thyme, stalks removed
sea salt and freshly ground black pepper
1–1.5kg corn-fed chicken
2 onions, unpeeled, sliced thickly
2 banana shallots, unpeeled and
   halved lengthways

Risotto
1 onion, peeled and finely chopped
2 banana shallots, peeled and finely
   chopped
2 tablespoons olive oil
2–3 sprigs fresh thyme, stalks removed
250g arborio or carnaroli rice
500ml chicken or vegetable stock *or* 250ml
   vegetable stock and 250ml dry white wine
30g mascarpone
30g Parmesan shavings
sea salt and freshly ground black pepper

1. Put the butternut squash, whole and unpeeled, in a pan of salted water. Cover and bring to the boil and then simmer for approximately 1 hour or until just tender. Remove with a slotted spoon and set aside to cool.

2. Preheat the oven to 190°C/Fan 170°C/Gas 5.

3. Prepare the lemon to flavour the chicken. Cut the lemon into 8 slices and put into a bowl. Add the honey, sprinkle over the thyme and season. Stir to combine and chill in the fridge for 5–10 minutes.

4. When the squash is cool enough to handle, cut in half lengthways and lay it, skin side down, in a roasting tin. Sprinkle with the olive oil and season to taste. Add the rosemary and thyme, and on each piece lay one of the halves of the garlic bulb. Roast in the preheated oven, basting from time to time, for 40–50 minutes or until golden brown.

5. Meanwhile, joint the legs and wings from the chicken, leaving the crown intact. (Use the chicken joints in another recipe.) Carefully peel away the skin, easing it away from the flesh with your fingers but leaving one end still attached. Lay the prepared lemon slices over the flesh, then pull the skin back to cover them and ease into place. Ensure that the flesh is completely covered by the skin.

6. Place the unpeeled sliced onions and shallots in the bottom of a roasting dish and place the prepared chicken on top. Roast alongside the squash in the preheated oven, basting from time to time, for 35–45 minutes or until cooked through and golden brown, with the juices running clear.

7. Cut the cooled butternut squash in half lengthways.

8. While the squash and chicken are roasting, make the risotto. In a large heavy-based frying pan, sauté the onion and shallots in a little olive oil until just soft but not coloured. Add the thyme and then stir in the risotto rice (which should be twice the amount of the weight of the onion and shallots). Toss well to ensure that each grain of rice is coated well with the oil, adding a little more if necessary.

9. Heat the stock, or stock and wine. When hot, ladle into the rice mixture one ladleful at a time. Once the liquid has been absorbed, add another until all the stock is used. Continue to do this for 20 minutes, stirring all the time over a gentle heat to prevent sticking. When cooked the rice should be al dente; do not overcook it.

10. To finish off the risotto, remove the squash from the oven, scoop out the seeds and discard. Reserve the cooked herbs. Chop one half of the squash into 3cm pieces and fold carefully into the rice, together with the mascarpone and Parmesan shavings. Season to taste. Cut the other squash half into 4 pieces.

11. Remove the chicken from the oven and cut it in half lengthways.

12. To assemble the dish, remove the cooked onion and shallot slices with a slotted spoon from the dish in which the chicken was cooked and place a portion in the middle of each hot serving plate. Cover with 2 pieces of squash. Spoon the risotto over the squash and place a chicken portion on the risotto. Garnish with a few sprigs of the cooked herbs and a drizzle of olive oil. Serve immediately.

Oven-glazed Beef Fillet 'Mich Mich'

Not only is Michelle the woman I love so much, but she also manages to please my appetite with this amazing dish. Use organic British beef ideally but just make sure it has been hung for 20 days which will provide you with incredible flavours. The steak here is being cooked medium rare. If you would like it well done, add another 15 minutes to the cooking time.

SERVES: 4
PREPARATION TIME: 25 MINUTES
COOKING TIME: 20–25 MINUTES

salt and freshly ground black pepper
4 x 180g fillet steaks
4 star anise
200ml red wine
2 teaspoons sugar
100ml extra-virgin olive oil
2–3 banana shallots, peeled and thinly
  sliced
20 red cherry tomatoes
sprinkle thyme leaves

3 bay leaves
10ml sherry vinegar
400g spinach
1 bunch fresh basil, torn
2–3 garlic cloves, peeled
100ml double cream
30g unsalted butter
12 slices strong Cheddar
pinch paprika

1. Preheat the oven to 180°C/Fan 160°C/Gas 4.

2. Heat a heavy-based pan. Season the steaks and seal on both sides for 3–4 minutes.

3. Then place them on a hob-proof baking tray and put to one side. Return the pan to the heat to deglaze.

4. Cook the residue on the bottom of the frying pan with the star anise, red wine and a teaspoon of sugar. Cook gently for about 12 minutes to reduce.

5. In the meantime heat another pan. When hot, add a dash of olive oil, followed by the shallots, and sweat for 2 minutes. Add the cherry tomatoes, thyme, a bay leaf, the remaining sugar, and vinegar. Cover with a lid and cook gently for 2 minutes. Remove the tomatoes from the pan and reserve, pouring the cooking liquor into the wine sauce.

6. Return the pan to the stove and add some olive oil. Throw in the spinach and basil, and season. Stir in one of the garlic cloves and cook for no more than a minute.

7. Use a sieve to drain the spinach and basil, pouring the cooking liquor into the red wine sauce. Press down hard on the spinach with the back of a spoon to make sure all the water is extracted.

8. When the wine sauce has reduced down to a quarter, add the cream and bring it almost to the boil (but do not allow to boil) and immediately remove from the heat.

9. Halve the 2 remaining garlic cloves, add to the sauce, along with the butter and allow to infuse. Whisk to incorporate the butter fully and adjust the seasoning.

10. Divide the spinach between the steak fillets and cover with the tomatoes that are in the pan. Finally lay the cheese slices on top and sprinkle with paprika. Bake in the preheated oven for 6–8 minutes.

11. Serve hot, accompanied by the sauce.

Do not allow the cream to boil, either when it is first added or when reheating. To ensure the beef is tender, bruise it with a meat mallet but do not tear the meat. If wished, add a little freshly grated nutmeg to the spinach. To prevent the tomatoes being overcooked, chill them for 10–15 minutes in the fridge before using.

Oven-roasted Lamb Cutlets Glazed with Roquefort

This is one of my signature dishes and has pleased many people for the last 15 years. It also allowed me to discover and work alongside two of the most amazing young British chefs – Chris Wheeler, who will always be like a brother to me and who I am fortunate to have known for almost 20 years, and another special friend who I hold in similar admiration, Richard Guest. Instead of Roquefort, you can use Stilton, which is what was in the original recipe. You can also use lamb caul fat instead of pig, or simply none at all but the result is quite different. This goes very well with lentil fricassee (see page 196).

SERVES: 4
PREPARATION TIME: 35 MINUTES
CHILLING TIME: 1 HOUR
COOKING TIME: 25 MINUTES

4 lamb cutlets, with the long bones
    trimmed
10ml olive oil
Mousse
1 raw chicken breast, chilled
1 medium egg white
200ml double cream
100g Roquefort, cubed
4 fresh basil leaves
4 large (30cm) squares of caul fat
    (available from your butcher)

Sauce
50ml white wine
1/2 teaspoon caster sugar
50ml water
splash olive oil
1 garlic clove, peeled and halved
salt and freshly ground black pepper
50ml double cream
10g butter
5g fresh tarragon, chopped

In order to make sure the lamb is very tender, give it a tap with the heel of your hand on a hard surface before cooking to break up the fibres. Ensure you don't put too much oil in the pan.

1. To make the mousse, take the chicken breast straight from the fridge and blitz in a blender or food processor with the egg white. Add the cream and blitz again. Put 1 tablespoon of the mixture on top of each of the lamb cutlets. Top the mousse with a cube of Roquefort and 1 basil leaf. Open out the caul fat and use to wrap the cutlets. Chill in the fridge for 1 hour.

2. Preheat the oven to 180°C/Fan 160°C/Gas 4.

3. Heat the olive oil in a deep, ovenproof frying pan and when hot seal the wrapped cutlets on the bottom. Take off the heat and roast in the preheated oven for about 12 minutes, or until golden brown and the mousse is firm to the touch.

4. Remove the cutlets from the oven and set aside, keeping them warm.

5. Remove the oil and fat from the roasting dish and return it to the heat to deglaze the pan.

6. Add the white wine, sugar, water, splash of olive oil and the garlic. Season to taste, stir to combine and cook gently to reduce by a third, roughly 10–15 minutes.

7. When it has reduced, add the cream, butter and tarragon. Bring to the boil and, just before the sauce reaches boiling point, remove the pan from the heat and stir in the oil left over from frying the lamb cutlets. Pass through a sieve and reheat if necessary. Pour over the cutlets and serve hot.

Iced Raspberry Soufflés with Vanilla and Yogurt

This recipe is a bit technical but definitely worthwhile. Only use very fresh raspberries because I don't believe in freezing twice. So that they don't crack in the cold, you will need 6 freezerproof cups or ramekins for this recipe. You could make one large soufflé instead.

SERVES: 6
PREPARATION TIME: 20 MINUTES
COOKING TIME: 4–6 MINUTES
FREEZING TIME: 3–4 HOURS (MINIMUM) OR OVERNIGHT

500ml fresh raspberries, plus extra
   for decoration
juice of 1/2 lemon
1 vanilla pod, halved lengthways
150g natural yogurt (or fromage blanc
   or mascarpone)

1 tablespoon water
190g caster sugar
4 large egg whites
300ml double cream
icing sugar

1. Using one of the cups or ramekins as a measure, cut 6 collars of greaseproof paper to fit around the outside of the cups or ramekins and standing 5cm above the rims. Secure with an elastic band.

2. In a blender or food processor, blitz the raspberries into a pulp with the lemon juice. Scrape out the vanilla seeds and add to the raspberries. Fold in the yogurt to combine.

3. Heat the water and the sugar until bubbles appear. Just before the syrup starts to colour, remove from the heat.

4. With an electric mixer, whisk the egg whites until stiff peaks are formed. Gradually pour in the sugar syrup and whisk at maximum speed for 15 minutes until cool and thick.

5. Whip the cream until it thickens. Add the raspberries to the sugar syrup, then fold in the cream. Pour into a piping bag and pipe evenly into the cups or ramekins so that it reaches the top of the greaseproof paper. Cover the tops with more greaseproof paper or cling film to prevent freezer burn.

6. Freeze for a minimum of 3–4 hours and a maximum of 12 hours.

7. Serve straight from the freezer by cutting the elastic band and peeling away the greaseproof paper. Decorate with extra raspberries and sprinkle with icing sugar.

If wished, replace the lemon juice with 50ml kirsch. This is equally good when made with other berries.

Baked Apple Soufflés with Chocolate and Kirsch Sauce

Granny Smith would be the best apple to use here because of the skin's resistance but you could also use Braeburn. Put a little oil under the apple to make sure it doesn't get attached to the tray.

SERVES: 4
PREPARATION TIME: 40 MINUTES
COOKING TIME: 25 MINUTES

120g raspberry jam
35ml kirsch
15g cornflour
4 very large baking apples
100g butter, softened
100g bitter chocolate, 70 per cent cocoa solids, grated

8 medium egg whites
300g white chocolate, broken into pieces
400ml double cream
100g caster sugar
icing sugar

1. Preheat the oven to 180°C/Fan 160°C/Gas 4.

2. Gently heat the jam until melted and add a splash of kirsch. In a small bowl, stir the cornflour into a little cold water until dissolved. Add to the jam, stir to combine and remove from the heat. Allow to cool.

3. Cut the tops off the baking apples and then hollow out the centres, keeping the bottoms intact, and discard the flesh. Turn the apples upside down and leave on a plate for 10 minutes to release the juices. Set in a greased ovenproof dish. Grease the insides with the butter and sprinkle them with the bitter chocolate.

4. Whisk the egg whites to the stiff peak stage. Carefully fold into the jam with a spatula. Spoon this into the apple cavities and score around the rim of the apple to release the filling from the edges, so that the filling will rise when baked.

5. Bake in the preheated oven for 8–10 minutes, or until the filling has risen fully.

6. Meanwhile, melt the white chocolate in a bain-marie or a bowl over a pan of simmering water. Do not allow the bottom of the bowl to touch the water. When melted, stir in the remaining kirsch and the cream. Pour into a serving jug.

7. Serve the apples hot and dusted with icing sugar. Offer the sauce separately.

The jam can be prepared ahead and kept in the fridge until needed.

When you empty the apples turn them over quickly in order to release excess juice and humidity.

Rich Dark and White Chocolate Fondants

This is an exciting and very controversial combination of two different chocolates. It keeps well in the freezer. You will need 4–6 dariole moulds or ramekin dishes (150ml capacity) for this recipe.

SERVES: 4–6
PREPARATION TIME: 15–20 MINUTES
CHILLING TIME: 2 HOURS
COOKING TIME: 8 MINUTES

butter for greasing
250g bitter chocolate, 70 per cent cocoa
 solids, broken into pieces
250g unsalted butter
5 medium eggs

5 medium egg yolks
125g caster sugar
145g plain flour
1 quantity iced white chocolate
 with whisky (see page 238)

1. Grease and base line 4–6 dariole moulds or ramekin dishes (150ml capacity).

2. Melt the chocolate and butter together in a bain-marie or a bowl over a pan of hot water, making sure that the bottom of the bowl does not touch the water. When melted and glossy, remove from the heat and allow to cool.

3. In a bowl, using an electric mixer, whisk together the eggs, egg yolks and sugar until thick and trebled in volume. When lifted, the whisk should leave a trail behind.

4. Using a metal spoon or spatula, carefully fold in the flour, making sure it is fully incorporated.

5. Fill the moulds or ramekins evenly. Push a frozen cube of white chocolate (see page 238) into the centre of each.

6. Chill in the fridge for at least 2 hours before cooking.

7. Just before you are ready for them, preheat the oven to 180°C/Fan 160°C/Gas 4.

8. Bake in the oven for 7 minutes and serve immediately.

Make sure that the eggs are at room temperature. If wished, add a few drops of kirsch at the same time as the white chocolate.

Whole Baked Oranges with Crème Brûlée

You could keep the two halves to attach together, so the finished result looks like the original. Make sure you take them out of the oven when they are still a bit wobbly.

SERVES: 8
PREPARATION TIME: 20–25 MINUTES
RESTING TIME: 1 HOUR
COOKING TIME: 50 MINUTES
INFUSION TIME: 12 HOURS

8 large oranges
100ml Cointreau or Grand Marnier
500ml milk
500ml double cream

10 egg yolks
200g caster sugar
50g brown demerara sugar, for glazing

1. Wash the oranges in hot water to remove the wax and then cut them in half and carefully squeeze out the juice without breaking the skins.

2. Scrape out the flesh from the oranges and discard it. Marinate the skins in Cointreau or Grand Marnier overnight. Remove with a slotted spoon and turn upside down to drain well, reserving the marinade. Set in an ovenproof dish.

3. Preheat the oven to 110°C/Fan 90°C/Gas ¼.

4. In a saucepan and on a low heat, reduce the orange juice to a syrup, roughly 30–40 minutes. Bring the milk and cream to the boil in a separate pan and then mix into the syrup.

5. Meanwhile, whisk the eggs. Add the caster sugar and continue whisking until they become pale and creamy.

6. Remove the milk and cream from the heat and pour into the whisked eggs. Stir well to combine and add the marinade.

7. Divide the filling equally between the oranges and bake in the preheated oven for 25–35 minutes, it should all still be wobbly. Preheat the grill to high.

8. Remove from the oven and allow to cool slightly. Leave to chill until ready to serve.

9. At the last minute, sprinkle with the brown sugar and glaze, either under the preheated grill or using a culinary blowtorch.

You could add ½ teaspoon of Cointreau to each orange before baking.

This recipe is also good with grapefruit, lemon, pineapple, mango, or anything else with a resisting thick skin.

Caramelised Pear and Cranberry Tarte Tatin

This recipe can be made using many different foods – from plums, apples, pineapples and strawberries to tomatoes and onions – as long as you make sure the puff pastry is wrapped tightly round and touching the caramel. This recipe was introduced on Hell's Kitchen and was very popular. Two of my best and favourite contestants mastered the result very well. They happened to be Kelly and Stein. You will need 12cm tart tins for this recipe, which can be prepared in advance, up to the end of step 7 and frozen.

SERVES: 4
PREPARATION TIME: 20 MINUTES
COOKING TIME: 30 MINUTES

3 vanilla pods, halved lengthways
4 tablespoons fresh cranberries, or thawed
    if frozen
2 tablespoons caster sugar
pinch ground cinnamon
4 Comice pears
70g ready-made puff pastry

Caramel
120g caster sugar
4–5 tablespoons water
To serve
4 scoops vanilla ice-cream
icing sugar
4 sprigs fresh mint

To make the recipe more simple, use thick honey instead of the caramel. Instead of ice-cream, you can use chilled low-fat crème fraîche.

1. Preheat the oven to 220°C/Fan 200°C/Gas 8.

2. Heat a heavy-based pan and when hot add two halves of the vanilla pods, cranberries and sugar. Cook for 2–3 minutes until the sugar has dissolved with the cranberries. Remove from the heat and allow to cool.

3. Cut four circles from greaseproof paper, larger than the tart tins. Scrunch them up and place in the bottom of the tins. Sprinkle each one with ground cinnamon and 1 of the vanilla pod halves.

4. To make the caramel, heat the 120g sugar and water in a heavy-based pan until it has melted and changed colour. Spoon the hot caramel into each circle of greaseproof paper and allow to cool for roughly 2 minutes.

5. Meanwhile, peel the pears. Carefully remove a thin slice from the base and cut and discard a third from the stalk end. Use a teaspoon to scoop out the inside of the pears, including the core. Fill with the cranberry compote.

6. Roll out the puff pastry to a thickness of 3mm and cut into 4 circles.

7. Place the tins with the set caramel upside down on top of the filled pears, and carefully turn them both over so that the tins are underneath. (The larger base of the pear should be touching the caramel.)

8. Cover the pears with the pastry, press tightly so that that no air is left underneath; the pastry should also be touching and pressed into the caramel. Chill in the fridge to rest for 20 minutes.

9. Bake for 15 minutes in the preheated oven. Remove and allow to rest for 5 minutes.

10. Return them to the hot oven and bake for a further 15 minutes.

11. Holding the greaseproof paper, carefully tip the pears upside down on to a serving plate and remove the greaseproof paper.

12. Top with vanilla ice-cream, dust with icing sugar and decorate with a sprig of mint. Serve immediately.

LATE SUPPER

My Own French Onion Soup
Camembert Bread
Home-dried Duck Carpaccio
Baked Vacherin Cheese with Iberico Ham
Fish Topped with Goat's Cheese Rarebit
Childhood Baked Stuffed Tomatoes
Aubergine Hummus
Cold Roast Piccalilli Chicken
Minute Steak with Tomato Relish
Late Piquant 'Minute' Chicken
Shepherd's Pie-style Baked Jacket Potatoes
Crispy Ham and Cheese Pork Chop
 Cappuccio

My Own French Onion Soup

This soup is streets ahead of other good, hearty soups and no book of mine would be the same without it. I use St André red onions but white onions will also do. If you do use sharp white onions, keep them in milk for several hours before cooking, which neutralises the acidity. This soup will keep in the fridge for 3 days and is so filling it can be served as a meal in itself.

SERVES: 4
PREPARATION TIME: 15 MINUTES
COOKING TIME: 50 MINUTES

150g unsalted butter
1 tablespoon olive oil
1kg red onions, thinly sliced
1 sprig fresh thyme, stalks removed
2 bay leaves
salt and freshly ground black pepper
3 teaspoons caster sugar
750ml dry white wine

350ml strong vegetable stock, hot
1 tablespoon lemon juice
Croûtons
1 baguette
1 garlic clove, peeled
180g Gruyère cheese, sliced
freshly ground black pepper
pinch paprika

1. Melt the butter in a large saucepan with the oil and gently cook the onions for about 6–8 minutes or until softened.

2. Add the herbs and seasoning, sprinkle over the sugar and cook for a further 5 minutes or until the onions are melting and glossy.

3. Pour in the wine and raise the heat. Bring back to the boil and simmer to reduce for 10 minutes.

4. Add the hot stock, bring back to the boil and simmer for 25 minutes.

5. When you are ready to serve the soup, preheat the grill. Slice the baguette diagonally and dry-fry in a heavy-based pan without oil or butter. While it is toasting, rub a clove of garlic on the bottom of the pan to infuse the bread.

6. When the baguette pieces are golden brown, top with the sliced cheese, grind over the pepper, sprinkle with the paprika, and grill for 2–3 minutes (or microwave for 10 seconds) until the cheese is bubbling.

7. Just before serving the soup, add the lemon juice and stir. Ladle into hot bowls and top with the cheesy croûtons. Serve immediately.

Before being grilled, the croûtons can be rolled up flat with a rolling pin to make them crispier.

The soup can be made in advance and reheated when needed – in fact, it improves the flavour. Warm it up slowly for 5 minutes but don't allow it to boil.

Camembert Bread

I think this is a masterpiece, perhaps the culmination of my career as a baker, and I can't count the number of people whom I have converted to bread-making through this recipe. It is a simple bread dough, but its combination with a good cheese makes it something special. I first learned to make this bread when I was introduced to the craft of baking as a fourteen-year-old. I felt like Alice in Wonderland, entering an unknown world, and it was the best job of my life. This is one of my signature dishes and I teach it at the Novelli Academy.

SERVES: 4
PREPARATION TIME: 45 MINUTES, PLUS 1 HOUR 40 MINUTES PROVING
FREEZER TIME: 10 MINUTES
COOKING TIME: 15–20 MINUTES
INFUSION TIME: 4 HOURS

Dough
375g strong white flour, warmed
1 heaped teaspoon salt
2–3 tablespoons olive oil
10g fast-action dried yeast
225ml warm water
2 teaspoons caster sugar
Cheese filling
1 x 250g whole mature Camembert or
  Vacherin or Toppenrose cheese
40ml chilli oil, or extra-virgin olive oil
  with a dash of Tabasco

1 garlic clove, peeled and halved
2–3 sprigs fresh sage, stalks removed
2–3 sprigs fresh thyme, stalks removed
1 bay leaf
30g green or black olive tapenade
freshly ground black pepper
2–3 tablespoons eau de vie
To serve
1 quantity walnut dip (see page 234)

1. First prepare the cheese filling. Put the cheese in the freezer for 10 minutes for the skin to become hard. Then, using a potato peeler, peel off and discard the skin. This way there is much less waste. Prick it with a fork. Combine the remaining filling ingredients in a suitable dish, add the cheese and leave to infuse in the fridge for 4 hours.

2. Warm the bowl of a mixer or food processor fitted with a dough hook. (If making by hand, warm a large mixing bowl.) Put all the dough ingredients into the warmed bowl and combine.

3. When the dough leaves the sides of the bowl, turn out on to a lightly floured surface and knead until smooth but not sticky. Place in a clean bowl, cover with a clean damp cloth or cling film and allow to prove in a warm place until doubled in size, about 45–60 minutes.

4. Turn out on to a lightly floured surface and knock back. Knead until smooth. The dough is now ready for use and at this stage could be used to make plain bread or rolls.

5. On a lightly floured surface, roll out the dough until large enough to wrap around the cheese. Drain the cheese, discarding the infusion liquid, and place in the centre of the dough. Seal the edges well; pull the edges over the top of the cheese, and press to seal. Turn over so that the joins are underneath and the top is smooth. Place on a baking tray and leave to prove until doubled in size, a good 40 minutes at room temperature. Spray lightly with water every 15 minutes, which keeps it moist and allows it to rise more quickly.

6. Preheat the oven to 220°C/Fan 200°C/Gas 7.

7. Sprinkle a little flour on top of the bread, then bake in the preheated oven for a good 5 minutes.

8. Reduce the heat to 160°C/Fan 140°C/Gas 3 and bake for another 10–13 minutes, or until golden brown and well risen. Tap the base of the loaf; if it sounds hollow, it is cooked.

9. Turn out on to a wire rack to cool and leave for 3–5 minutes before cutting into quarters. Serve with the walnut dip.

Home-dried Duck Carpaccio

This is a recipe I have always used, and although it takes time and must be prepared well in advance, it really is worth it. It makes a nice little appetiser when friends come round for a drink and is particularly good served on a baguette with rémoulade (see page 228).

SERVES: 4
PREPARATION TIME: 25 MINUTES
MARINATING TIME: 8–12 HOURS
DRYING TIME: 1 MONTH

1 large fresh duck breast
100g rock salt
25g caster sugar
about 10 juniper berries, crushed
2 dried bay leaves, crushed

1 teaspoon olive oil
1 small sprig fresh thyme, stalks removed
To serve
handful of mixed salad leaves
Monique basic dressing (see page 222)

1. In a hot pan, dry-fry the duck breast, skin side down, until the fat runs. Remove from the pan with a slotted spoon, reserving the juices, and place in a dish. Mix the duck fat with the rock salt and sugar (this enhances the flavour), and spread it over and around the duck, together with the juniper berries and bay leaves. Cover loosely, and leave to marinate in a cool place for 8–12 hours.

2. Wash off the salt and dry the breast with kitchen paper. Rub the olive oil over it and leave for 10 minutes. Make 5–6 cuts into the fat of the breast, and insert the thyme leaves into the cuts.

3. Wrap the breast in muslin, tie with string, and hang in a cool dry place, with air circulating around it (e.g. a cool larder, utility room, or garage) for 1 month. Put a container or plate underneath, to catch any juices that might be produced after 3 weeks or so.

4. Remove from the muslin. Thinly slice the breast – it should be as thin as dried ham – and fan around each serving plate. Toss the mixed salad leaves in with the dressing, season and place in the middle of the carpaccio.

When the duck breast has dried, it will keep in the fridge virtually for ever, just like salami. Simply change the cling film every time you slice off some flesh. When drying it will release an oily liquid, which you can use in the dressing.

Baked Vacherin Cheese with Iberico Ham

Here is an unusual marinated cheese recipe. Wrapped in Iberico ham and cooked to perfection, it is one of the most popular dishes at my gastropub 'Touch of Novelli' and also a favourite of my co-partners at The White Horse, Harry Nugent and Tony McFarland.

SERVES: 4–6
PREPARATION TIME: 15 MINUTES
FREEZING TIME: 20 MINUTES
COOKING TIME: 10 MINUTES
MARINATING TIME: 12 HOURS

1 Vacherin cheese, in its box
50ml cognac or brandy, or very dry
   white wine
1 tablespoon tapenade
1 sprig fresh thyme, used whole
1 sprig fresh rosemary, used whole
1 garlic clove, sliced thinly

½ teaspoon paprika
salt and freshly ground black pepper
4–5 fresh basil leaves
4 large thin slices Iberico ham
100ml redcurrant jelly
juice of ½ lemon

1. Unwrap the cheese but do not discard the wrapping. Turn it upside down and return to the box. Prick with a fork a few times and pour on the cognac or brandy. Spread with tapenade and place the thyme, rosemary and garlic on top, dust with paprika and season well.

2. Cover the cheese with its wrapping, replace the lid and leave to marinate for 12 hours in the fridge.

3. Preheat the oven to 200°C/Fan 180°C/Gas 6.

4. Remove from the box. Place the basil leaves on top and wrap in the Iberico ham. Return to the box and freeze for 20 minutes.

5. Still in its box, place on a baking tray and bake in the preheated oven for 10 minutes.

6. Meanwhile, heat the redcurrant jelly in a saucepan. When it has melted, add the lemon juice and pour into a serving dish.

7. Remove the cheese from the oven and unwrap. Serve hot with the warm redcurrant sauce on some warm crusty bread.

When marinating the cheese do this at room temperature to help the flavours be absorbed.

Fish Topped with Goat's Cheese Rarebit

A very quick way to serve fish, this is my version of the original Welsh rarebit topping, which has blown my mind for many years. It works very well with haddock, cod, or sole.

SERVES: 2
PREPARATION TIME: 5–6 MINUTES
COOKING TIME: 8–10 MINUTES

10g butter
10g plain flour, sifted
½ teaspoon Dijon mustard
70ml beer (Bishop's Finger cask bitter)
50ml double cream

salt and freshly ground black pepper
100g goat's cheese, crumbled
1 medium egg yolk
1 tablespoon fresh chives, snipped
2 x 6–8oz white fish fillets, e.g. cod or halibut

1. Preheat the oven to 180°C/Fan 160°C/Gas 4.

2. Melt the butter in a pan and stir in the flour. Cook for 1 minute.

3. Add the Dijon mustard, pour in the beer and cream, and season to taste. Add the goat's cheese and allow to melt, stirring constantly at a low heat.

4. When the cheese has melted, remove from the heat and allow to cool slightly, for roughly 3 minutes. Stir in the egg yolk and chives.

5. Cover each fish fillet with the cooled topping and bake in the preheated oven until the fish has cooked and the glaze has coloured. Depending on the thickness of the fillet this should take 5–8 minutes. Serve hot.

Make sure the sauce has cooled well before adding the egg yolk, as otherwise it may scramble. In place of the Bishop's Finger beer, use your own favourite tipple.

Childhood Baked Stuffed Tomatoes

This recipe conjures up many pleasant childhood memories. Use large, firm but ripe beef tomatoes and stuff, as here, with a savoury minced beef mixture and top with a little cheese. This dish was inspired by my mother.

SERVES: 4
PREPARATION TIME: 15–20 MINUTES
COOKING TIME: 25–30 MINUTES

4 beef tomatoes
4 tablespoons extra-virgin olive oil
2 teaspoons cumin seeds
100g shallots or onions, peeled and diced
2 teaspoons caster sugar
1 tablespoon tomato purée
1 teaspoon Tabasco
4 sprigs fresh thyme, stalks removed and chopped

10–12 fresh basil leaves, torn
100ml dry white wine
400g lean minced beef
2 garlic cloves, peeled and chopped
salt and freshly ground black pepper
100g cheese (Gruyère or Emmenthal), sliced

1. Preheat the oven to 160°C/Fan 140°C/Gas 3.

2. Cut a slice off the top of each tomato with a sharp knife and carefully remove the flesh. Take care not to cut through the skin. Reserve the shells and set aside.

3. Heat the flesh in a pan. Add a dash of olive oil and the cumin seeds. Bring to the boil and add the shallots or onions, sugar, tomato purée, Tabasco, thyme and half the basil, and sweat gently for 3–5 minutes.

4. Pour in the white wine and stir in the beef. Reduce the heat, cover and cook for a further 5 minutes. Add the garlic and remaining basil leaves, and stir to combine.

5. Season the tomato shells and place on a baking tray. Spoon in the beef and bake in the preheated oven for 10–12 minutes.

6. Remove from the oven, top with the cheese and return to the oven to bake for a further 5 minutes. Serve hot.

Beef tomatoes are definitely the best. As soon as they are scooped, turn the tomatoes over to release the excess juice.

Aubergine Hummus

This is an alternative to ordinary hummus. Made from aubergines, herbs and spices, it is delicious served warm with a crusty, rustic bread of your choice.

SERVES: 4
PREPARATION TIME: 10 MINUTES
COOKING TIME: 20–25 MINUTES

2 large aubergines
3 garlic cloves, peeled, halved and core removed
15–20g caster sugar
1 teaspoon Cajun spices
2 sprigs fresh thyme
225ml olive oil

salt and freshly ground black pepper
200g chickpeas, cooked and drained
30ml tahini
a good handful fresh coriander, chopped
a good handful fresh basil, chopped
juice of 1–2 lemons

1. Preheat the oven to 180°C/Fan 160°C/Gas 4.

2. Cut the aubergines in half. Dice 1 garlic clove and scatter over the aubergine. Sprinkle with the sugar and Cajun spice.

3. Lay the thyme on top and drizzle over 25ml of the olive oil.

4. Place on a baking tray, season, cover with foil and bake in the preheated oven for 20–25 minutes, or until soft.

5. Remove from the oven and leave to cool. When cool enough to handle, scoop out the flesh, discarding the skins. Blitz in a blender or food processor. Add the chickpeas, the remaining garlic, tahini, coriander, basil and lemon juice, and blitz together until smooth.

6. Gradually pour the remaining olive oil in through the funnel on to the rotating blades until it takes on the consistency of mayonnaise. You may not need all the oil.

7. Adjust the seasoning and chill until required.

If you wish or if time is short, use canned, drained chickpeas. If you don't have tahini, add another lemon.

Cold Roast Piccalilli Chicken

Serve this chicken and piccalilli with a contrasting salad and French bread for lunch, dinner or even picnics.

SERVES: 4–6
PREPARATION TIME: 15 MINUTES
COOKING TIME: 45–60 MINUTES
COOLING TIME: 1 HOUR

1 large chicken
150–200ml piccalilli, store-bought or see
   page 229
2 onions, peeled and quartered

4 sprigs fresh thyme
3 bay leaves
salt and freshly ground black pepper
10ml olive oil

1. Preheat the oven to 180°C/Fan 160°C/Gas 4.

2. Separate the skin from the breast of the chicken by slowly pushing your hand under the skin, being careful not to tear it. When there is enough space for you to flatten your hand under the skin, spread the piccalilli over the flesh, creating an even layer. Ease the skin back over the flesh and tuck it in.

3. Place the onions, thyme and bay leaves in the cavity of the chicken. Season the outside well, and drizzle with olive oil.

4. In a deep ovenproof frying pan with a lid, heat some more olive oil and brown the chicken all over.

5. When it is browned, cover the pan with a lid or foil, and bake in the preheated oven for 45 minutes, depending on the weight of the chicken.

6. Remove from the oven and leave to cool for 1 hour.

7. When cold, cover with cling film and chill in the fridge until required. Serve cold in slices.

When pushing your fingers under the skin to introduce the piccalilli, make sure you don't pierce the skin: keep it intact like a pocket.

Minute Steak with Tomato Relish

This is one of Mandy's (Michelle's mum) treats and it is, believe it or not, one of the foods I enjoy most. It is especially good after a very long, stressful day. Look out for 21-day matured beef at the butcher's or on the supermarket shelves. The meat will have a good flavour and generally be very tender. This recipe will cook the meat to medium rare.

SERVES: 1
PREPARATION TIME: 5 MINUTES
COOKING TIME: 15 MINUTES

150g sirloin steak, trimmed of all fat
salt and freshly ground black pepper
20ml balsamic vinegar
20cm baguette

2 tablespoons mayonnaise, for spreading
1 quantity tomato relish (see page 221)
30g Cheddar cheese, sliced

1. Preheat the oven to 180°C/Fan 160°C/Gas 4. Cut the steak in half and season well.

2. Bake the baguette in the preheated oven for 5–10 minutes or until warmed through and crispy.

3. Meanwhile, heat a heavy-based frying pan. When hot, add the steak and cook for 1 minute. Turn over, add the balsamic vinegar and then cook for a further 2 minutes.

4. Remove the baguette from the oven and cut in half lengthways. Spread both the cut sides with mayonnaise. Spread a little tomato relish on one side only and cover with the steak. Lay the cheese on top, cover with the other half and serve immediately.

To keep the baguette together when serving, pin it together with cocktail sticks.

Late Piquant 'Minute' Chicken

The beauty of this recipe is that it creates its own flavoursome stock, which can then be served with freshly cooked rice. This is quicker to make than any takeaway recipe and you don't have to wait for delivery. Make sure you use a jumbo cucumber.

SERVES: 4–6
PREPARATION TIME: 10–15 MINUTES
COOKING TIME: 30 MINUTES

4 chicken breasts
2 tablespoons olive oil
1 garlic clove, peeled and chopped
2 bay leaves
small bunch of fresh thyme, chopped
1 teaspoon Tabasco
2 tablespoons tomato purée
2 tablespoons sun-dried tomato purée
200g small cap mushrooms, wiped and halved
juice of 1 lemon
2 teaspoons caster sugar
1 teaspoon English mustard
1 litre double cream

4 gherkins, drained and sliced
50g fresh mixed herbs (e.g. tarragon, parsley and coriander), chopped
salt and freshly ground black pepper
Rice
2 tablespoons olive oil
1 onion, peeled and chopped
1 bay leaf
3 sprigs fresh thyme
300g long-grain rice
pinch freshly grated nutmeg
450ml water/chicken or vegetable stock, warmed

1. First, prepare the rice. Heat a large saucepan, add the olive oil and gently sweat the onion for 1–2 minutes.

2. Add the bay leaf, thyme, rice and nutmeg. Stir well to coat the rice, then add the water or stock. Cover the pan with crumpled greaseproof paper, which acts as a lid but by allowing steam to escape it stops the rice from burning, and cook gently for about 20–30 minutes or until the stock has been absorbed into the rice. Remove the thyme and bay leaves.

3. Meanwhile, prepare the chicken. Skin and slice into 3cm pieces. Heat the oil in a frying pan and sauté the garlic for 1 minute. Add the bay leaves and thyme. When the pan is hot, stir in the chicken and cook over a moderate to high heat for 2 minutes to seal it.

4. Stir in the Tabasco, both tomato purées, the mushrooms, lemon juice, sugar, mustard, double cream and gherkins. Stir in the mixed herbs and season to taste.

5. To serve, place spoonfuls of rice on to hot serving plates and top with the chicken.

Shepherd's Pie-style Baked Jacket Potatoes

An unusual way to serve jacket potatoes, this dish is actually very similar to shepherd's pie. I use Maris Piper potatoes and, since it is not always possible to buy fresh chicken livers, frozen will do – once thawed they work just as well.

SERVES: 4
PREPARATION TIME: 20–25 MINUTES
COOKING TIME: 1 HOUR 20 MINUTES–1 HOUR 40 MINUTES

2 large jacket potatoes (300g each)
20ml olive oil
salt and freshly ground black pepper
½ quantity olive oil mash (see page 195)
200g chicken livers, thawed if frozen
½ onion, peeled and diced
1 garlic clove, peeled and crushed

1 bay leaf
3 sprigs fresh thyme, stalks removed
pinch caster sugar
½ teaspoon tomato purée
10ml brandy
50ml double cream
8 slices Cheddar cheese

1. Preheat the oven to 180°C/Fan 160°C/Gas 4.

2. Prepare the jacket potatoes. Rub with half the olive oil and season. Place on a baking tray and bake in the preheated oven for 40–60 minutes, depending on size.

3. Remove the potatoes from the oven and scoop out about two thirds of the flesh. Reserve the jackets but use the potato flesh to make the ½ quantity of olive oil mash (see page 195).

4. Trim the chicken livers if necessary and dice into 4mm pieces.

5. Pour a little of the oil into a pan, heat and gently cook the onion, garlic, bay leaf and thyme for 2–3 minutes. Season and add the sugar.

6. Raise the heat and when hot add the chicken livers. Cook for about 1 minute until sealed.

7. Add the tomato purée and cook for 1 minute.

8. Add the brandy, flambé it, and then add the cream (make sure it is not too runny).

9. Divide the mash between the jackets, then the livers, and finally top with the cheese. Return to the hot oven and bake until the cheese is golden brown.

Instead of the chicken livers, you can use minced beef or lamb.

You can marinate the chicken livers in the brandy for 6 hours in advance. Drain from the marinade before cooking.

Crispy Ham and Cheese
Pork Chop Cappuccio

A nice and original way to cook pork, try to use organic, or you could substitute it with veal, smoked ham or smoked salmon. The idea is similar to the old favourite 'cordon bleu'. It can be served simply with a mixed salad or even with a fried quail egg.

SERVES: 4
PREPARATION TIME: 25 MINUTES
COOKING TIME: 20 MINUTES

4 pork chops
1 teaspoon salt
1 teaspoon freshly ground black pepper
4 slices Swiss cheese
4 slices cooked ham
seasoned flour
fresh breadcrumbs, very fine
knob butter, for frying
juice of ½ lemon
Egg wash
1–2 medium egg yolks
1 teaspoon cold water

pinch salt
Cappuccio sauce
20g tomato purée
20g capers
2 tablespoons vinegar
50ml white wine
150ml double cream
salt and Szechuan pepper
pinch of caster sugar
Garnish
sprig fresh chervil

1. Preheat the oven to 170°C/Fan 150°C/Gas 3.

2. With a sharp knife, remove the bone from the pork chop. Lay the chop between two doubled sheets of cling film and beat with a rolling pin until even in thickness.

3. Season on both sides. Place the cheese and ham slices on top.

4. Make the egg wash by beating together the ingredients. Coat the pork with seasoned flour, then the egg wash and finally the breadcrumbs.

5. Heat the butter in a frying pan and seal the meat on both sides. Squeeze over the lemon juice and transfer to a baking dish. Bake in the preheated oven for 20 minutes.

6. Using the pan that the pork has been fried in, make the sauce by stirring in the tomato purée, capers, vinegar and wine. Add the cream, seasoning and a touch of sugar and warm through.

7. Garnish with the chervil and serve with new potatoes and salad or vegetables.

Choose Beaufort if you want a stronger flavour cheese.

REPERTOIRE

Pommes Boulangère Maman Novelli
Gratin Dauphinois à la Jean de Vienne
Real Roast Potatoes
Olive Oil Mash
Lentil Fricassee
Vegetable Nage
Pain de Mie
Ricotta Gnocchi
Pilaf Rice
Risotto
Choux Paste
Tuille Biscuits
Pancakes
Aromatic Cream Sauce
Butter with a Piquant Twist
Butter Cream Sauce
Proper Tomato Sauce
Tomato Relish
Monique Basic Dressing
Anchovyade
Onion Marmalade
Rémoulade
Piccalilli
Fresh Herb Oil
Walnut Dip
Stock Syrup
Crème Pâtissière
Coconut Cream
Iced White Chocolate with Whisky

Pommes Boulangère Maman Novelli

This classic potato dish was handed down by my mother who used to make it for all the family. Now, I hope that you will create and enjoy this recipe too. It was always very popular in the winter, especially when served with lamb or veal cutlets. If you like, you can even layer the cutlets with the potatoes and cook it all together.

SERVES: 4
PREPARATION TIME: 15 MINUTES
COOKING TIME: 45 MINUTES

5–6 leaves Savoy cabbage
450g floury potatoes (e.g. Maris Piper)
25g butter
2 tablespoons olive oil
2 large onions, peeled and sliced
3 garlic cloves, peeled and chopped
4 sprigs fresh thyme, stalks removed
  and chopped

2 bay leaves
750ml–1 litre hot strong and rich chicken
  or vegetable stock
salt and freshly ground black pepper
200g Red Leicester cheese, sliced

1. Preheat the oven to 190°C/Fan 170°C/Gas 5. Grease an ovenproof dish.

2. Heat a pan of salted water. When boiling, blanch the cabbage leaves for 1 minute. Remove with a slotted spoon and drain.

3. Peel the potatoes and slice thinly, about 3mm thick, with a mandolin or sharp knife.

4. Heat the butter and olive oil in a heavy-based frying pan.

5. Sweat the onions, garlic, thyme and bay leaves for 2–3 minutes or until softened.

6. Layer the potatoes, onions and cabbage alternately in the prepared dish, with a final layer of potatoes.

7. Pour in the hot stock, enough to cover all the potatoes. Season to taste.

8. Bake, uncovered to allow the stock to evaporate, in the preheated oven for 45 minutes.

9. Remove from the oven 10 minutes before the end of the cooking time (the potato should feel soft when a knife is inserted into the dish) and place the cheese on top. Return to the hot oven and bake until golden brown and cooked through. Serve hot.

Use cabbage leaves from the inside as the outer ones are too thick.

Gratin Dauphinois à la Jean de Vienne

This is definitely the best potato gratin recipe in the world. It is another classic that can be served with any roast meats or fish of your choice. Always use the best ingredients that you can afford. This is the only recipe that my dad learned from his mum, my grandmother Louise, who was another fabulous cook.

SERVES: 4
PREPARATION TIME: 25 MINUTES
COOKING TIME: 45–60 MINUTES

1kg floury potatoes (e.g. King Edward, Maris Piper or Desirée)
500ml double cream
3–4 garlic cloves, peeled and chopped
freshly grated nutmeg to taste
100ml full-fat milk

2 sprigs fresh thyme
2 bay leaves
salt and freshly ground black pepper
300g strong cheese (Cheddar, Emmenthal, Gruyère or Beaufort), grated

1. Preheat the oven to 160°C/Fan 140°C/Gas 2.

2. Peel the potatoes and slice thinly, about 2–3mm thick, using a mandolin or sharp knife.

3. Pour the cream into a heavy pan and add the garlic. Stir in the nutmeg and warm through.

4. Add the potatoes, followed by the milk, thyme and bay leaves. Stir well and season to taste.

5. Lightly grease a large gratin dish. Layer the potatoes with two thirds of the grated cheese. Sprinkle the remaining cheese over the final layer of potato.

6. Bake in the preheated oven for 45–60 minutes or until golden brown and tender.

7. Serve hot as a side dish to roasted meat or poultry.

Do not wash the potatoes as you will lose their vital starch. If the cream begins to split, it is a sign that the oven is too hot, so reduce the heat a little. To make a curried dauphinois, add 1 tablespoon medium curry powder at step 3.

Real Roast Potatoes

This recipe always works and will give you perfect, crispy roast potatoes every time. The secret lies in not washing off the starch.

SERVES: 6
PREPARATION TIME: 15 MINUTES
COOKING TIME: 45 MINUTES

2kg floury potatoes (e.g. Maris Piper or King Edward)
300ml olive oil
1–2 garlic bulbs, halved

3–4 sprigs whole fresh rosemary
1 teaspoon rock salt
1 teaspoon cracked black pepper
4 bay leaves

1. Preheat the oven to 220°C/Fan 200°C/Gas 7. Place a baking tray in the oven to preheat.

2. Peel the potatoes and cut in half. Put the remaining ingredients in a bowl and stir to combine. Add the potatoes and stir again to coat thoroughly.

3. Turn on to the preheated baking tray and roast in the preheated oven for 20 minutes.

4. Reduce the heat to 180°C/Fan 160°C/Gas 4 and roast for a further 25 minutes. Serve immediately.

In place of the oil, I like to use beef dripping for its superior flavour, but you can also use duck fat.

Olive Oil Mash

A great alternative to simple mashed potato, make this in advance and keep it warm until you're ready to use it.

SERVES: 3–4
PREPARATION TIME: 15 MINUTES
COOKING TIME: 25 MINUTES, PLUS 30 MINUTES RESTING

120ml double cream
1 teaspoon caster sugar
250ml olive oil
100ml chicken or vegetable stock, hot
1 garlic clove, peeled and diced
½ onion, peeled and diced

1 bay leaf
2 sprigs thyme, stalks removed and chopped
600g new potatoes, scrubbed and skins left on
salt and freshly ground black pepper

1. Heat the cream, sugar, olive oil, stock, garlic, onion, bay leaf and thyme together. Bring to the boil, then remove from the heat, cover and leave to stand undisturbed for 30 minutes.

2. Meanwhile, boil the potatoes in their skins for 20–25 minutes. Drain and leave to cool slightly.

3. When cool enough to handle, use the back of a knife to scrape away the skins. Pass the potatoes through a fine sieve or potato ricer.

4. Pass the cream through a sieve. Pour into a clean pan and reheat.

5. When hot, pour over the potatoes. Stir to combine, season to taste and serve immediately.

To enrich this recipe, add 50g butter to the cream at step 4. For a different flavour, use the same amount of a flavoured oil (sundried tomato, garlic, chilli or curry).

Lentil Fricassee

A great source of energy and a fantastic substitute for your normal carbohydrates.

SERVES 6
PREPARATION TIME: 1 HOUR 15 MINUTES
COOKING TIME: 45–55 MINUTES

200g green lentils
800ml vegetable stock
1 tablespoon olive oil
2 large carrots, peeled and diced
1 onion, peeled and diced
4 stalks celery, diced

1 whole sprig rosemary
1 sprig thyme, stalk removed
1 bay leaf
1 bunch chervil, chopped
salt and freshly ground black pepper

1. Put the lentils in a bowl and cover in cold water. Leave to soak for 1 hour or until all the water has been absorbed.

2. Place the lentils in a saucepan and pour over the stock. Leave to bubble away until the lentils are cooked.

3. Splash the olive oil into a frying pan and add the carrots, onion, celery and herbs (except the chervil). Season and cook the vegetables until soft.

4. Just before needed, combine the vegetables and the lentils, stir through a bunch of fresh chervil and serve.

Vegetable Nage

This should be left to infuse for at least a day before using. It can be frozen in bags or glass containers. Defrost before using.

MAKES: 2–3 LITRES
PREPARATION TIME: 15 MINUTES
COOKING TIME: 2 MINUTES
INFUSION TIME: 12 HOURS

1.25kg white onions, peeled
1.3kg carrots, peeled
1.4kg leeks, trimmed and washed
700g celery sticks
1 orange, cut in half
1 lemon, cut in half
3 star anise
freshly ground black pepper
25g salt
4 bay leaves

5 white peppercorns
5 pink peppercorns
2 sprigs fresh thyme
2.5 litres water
750ml dry white wine
3 sprigs fresh tarragon
6 sprigs fresh chervil, chopped
3 sprigs coriander
6 sprigs fresh flat-leaf parsley
1 garlic bulb, crushed and sliced in half

1. Peel, wash and chop all the vegetables into 5mm dice. (This is essential, so that all the flavour is extracted quickly.)

2. Turn all the vegetables and fruit into a large pan. Add the star anise, pepper, salt, bay leaves, peppercorns and thyme. Add the water and bring to the boil.

3. Just as the water comes to the boil, add the white wine. Bring back to the boil for 10 seconds only and remove from the heat.

4. Add the remaining fresh herbs and the remaining ingredients. Stir well to combine and infuse for 12 hours at room temperature.

5. Pass through a colander, then a fine sieve or strainer.

6. Pack into freezer bags or containers, according to portion size, and freeze.

Pain de Mie

This is a very nostalgic recipe for me that I used to make when I was a baker, back home in my local bakery. This dough makes ideal bread for slicing into sandwiches, like croque madame on page 22. You will need a food processor or mixer, fitted with a dough hook.

MAKES: 2 X 1KG LOAVES
PREPARATION TIME: 1 HOUR
COOKING TIME: 20-25 MINUTES

250ml milk
250ml water
1kg strong plain flour, sifted and warmed
20g salt

50g caster sugar
80g unsalted butter, softened
25g powdered milk
60g fresh yeast or 40g dried yeast

1. Heat the milk and water together until at blood heat. Remove from the heat.

2. Warm the bowl of a mixer or food processor fitted with a dough hook. (If making by hand, warm a large mixing bowl.) Add the flour, salt, sugar, butter and powdered milk.

3. When the milk is tepid, add the creamed yeast or sprinkle on the dried yeast. Stir to combine.

4. Turn into the warmed bowl with the flour and combine until a dough is formed, making sure the dough does not stick to the bowl. If it does, add a touch more flour.

5. Knead the dough, for roughly 5 minutes, and divide between 2 x 1kg loaf tins.

6. Leave in a warm place to rise until doubled in size, roughly 40 minutes. Preheat the oven to 180°C/Fan 160°C/Gas 4.

7. Spray the loaves lightly with water every 15 minutes, which keeps them moist and allows them to rise more quickly.

8. Sprinkle a little flour on top of the loaves and bake in the preheated oven for 20–25 minutes. Check whether the loaves are cooked by tapping the bottom. If the bread sounds hollow, it's cooked. Leave to cool on a wire tray.

Make sure the milk is at no more than blood temperature when adding the yeast, as heat will kill it.

Ricotta Gnocchi

This is my grandmother's version of Italian gnocchi. As you can see, it is simple to make and it is also delicious to eat.

SERVES: 4–6
PREPARATION TIME: 35–40 MINUTES
COOKING TIME: 10 MINUTES

1kg potatoes (e.g. Desirée), unpeeled
175g plain flour, sifted, plus a little extra
¼–½ teaspoon salt

¼ teaspoon freshly ground white pepper
3 medium egg yolks, beaten
100g ricotta cheese

1. Preheat the oven to 200°C/180°C/Gas 4.

2. Boil the potatoes in their skins until just cooked, about 30 minutes. To check whether they are cooked, insert a knife and it should go through easily.

3. Drain the potatoes, then cut in half and place on a baking tray. Put in the preheated oven to dry for 4–6 minutes.

4. When cool enough to handle, scoop out the flesh, discarding the skins, turn into a bowl and mash well until there are no lumps.

5. Add the flour, salt, pepper, egg and ricotta cheese, and stir until just combined.

6. With a piping bag or using flour-coated hands, mould into long cigar shapes, approximately 1cm thick.

7. Cut into 2cm lengths and mark with the back of a fork to form a pattern.

8. Bring a pan of lightly salted water to the boil, add the gnocchi, bring back to the boil and simmer for 5 minutes or until the cooked gnocchi rise to the surface.

9. Drain well and serve immediately. If, however, you would like to keep them for later use, refresh the gnocchi in iced water after draining, and then drain again. Place them flat on a cloth and the gnocchi will keep for up to 3 days in the fridge covered with cling film.

10. To serve, pan fry in olive oil, fresh thyme, garlic and paprika.

Take care not to overprocess the potatoes, otherwise they will become gluey.

Pilaf Rice

This recipe ensures the rice is nice and moist and properly cooked every time.

SERVES: 4
PREPARATION TIME: 5 MINUTES
COOKING TIME: 25–30 MINUTES

2 tablespoons olive oil
4 shallots, peeled and diced
3 sprigs fresh thyme, stalks removed and chopped
1 bay leaf
½ teaspoon cumin seeds
1 garlic clove, peeled and crushed

300g long-grain rice
20g butter
freshly grated nutmeg, to taste
salt and freshly ground black pepper
50ml dry white wine
450ml chicken or vegetable stock, hot

1. Preheat the oven to 180°C/Fan 160°C/Gas 4.

2. Heat the oil in a heavy ovenproof pan with a lid. Add the shallots, thyme, bay leaf, cumin and garlic. Sweat on a low heat for about 2–3 minutes, or until the shallots are just soft but not coloured.

3. Stir in the rice, butter and nutmeg, and season to taste.

4. Pour in the wine, raise the heat and reduce by half. This should take about 5–6 minutes.

5. Pour in the stock. Cover the pan with a lid or foil, and bake in the preheated oven for 15–20 minutes. Serve hot.

To vary, use a little curry powder in place of the nutmeg.

Risotto

There's no real way to take short cuts with perfect risotto. Make sure you use arborio (risotto) rice and that the stock is hot in order to get excellent results every time. And stir as much as possible to allow the starch to be released from the grain.

SERVES: 2
PREPARATION TIME: 5–10 MINUTES
COOKING TIME: 25–30 MINUTES

25g unsalted butter
25ml olive oil
100g onions, diced
2 garlic cloves, peeled and chopped
6 sprigs fresh thyme, stalks removed
    and chopped

300g arborio or carnaroli risotto rice
salt and freshly ground black pepper
220ml dry white wine
600ml strong vegetable or chicken stock, hot

1. Melt the butter and oil in a large frying pan. Add the onions and sweat gently for 3 minutes or until softened, but do not allow to brown.

2. Add the garlic and thyme, and stir in the rice. Season and cook, stirring, for 2 minutes to coat the rice.

3. Pour in the white wine, a quarter at a time, and continue to cook, stirring constantly, until completely absorbed.

4. Pour in the hot stock gradually, a ladleful at a time, stirring gently until fully absorbed before adding the next. Don't try to rush it. Cook it slowly on a low heat and use a wooden spoon (which is less likely to break the risotto rice than a metal one).

5. Stir constantly until the rice is just cooked or al dente, about 25–30 minutes. Remove the thyme and serve immediately.

If wished, add ½ garlic clove, finely chopped, and herbs to taste. To vary the recipe, add 200g cooked vegetables (e.g. squash, pumpkins, courgettes, etc). If liked, add 50–80g of butter with a piquant twist (see page 218).

Choux Paste

A good basic recipe for sweet and savoury dishes. Make sure all the humidity has dried out from the paste before slowly adding your eggs.

SERVES: 4
PREPARATION TIME: 5–10 MINUTES
COOKING TIME: 15 MINUTES

250ml water
100g unsalted butter
pinch sugar
pinch salt
150g strong plain flour
4 medium eggs

Egg wash
1–2 medium egg yolks
1 teaspoon cold water
pinch salt

1. Preheat the oven to 180°C/Fan 160°C/Gas 4. Prepare a baking tray with baking parchment. Make the egg wash by beating the ingredients together. Set aside.

2. Pour the water into a large saucepan and add the butter, sugar and salt. Turn up the heat and the second that the butter has melted, turn down the heat and add the flour all at once, stirring constantly with a wooden spoon. When the flour is amalgamated, roughly 5 minutes, and the paste is smooth, remove from the heat.

3. With the pan off the heat, continue to stir for about 3–5 minutes or until the paste is just warm, but do not overbeat.

4. Add the eggs one at a time, beating after each addition until well incorporated before adding the next.

5. If making choux buns or eclairs, turn the mix into a piping bag and pipe on to the prepared baking tray, spaced about 5cm apart to allow for spreading.

6. Glaze the tops with the egg wash.

7. Bake in the preheated oven for about 15 minutes, depending on the size, until they have risen and are golden brown. Allow to cool on a wire tray.

For a crispy profiterole, leave them to dry for longer in the oven, or for a good 10 minutes in a low heat oven.

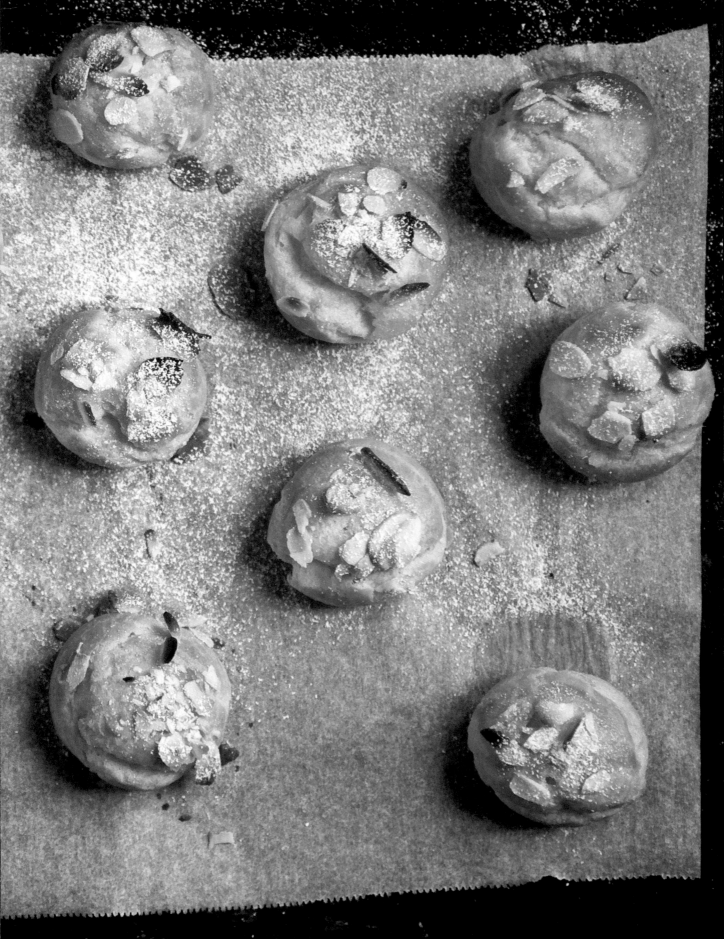

Tuille Biscuits

A great recipe for getting the kids involved.

MAKES: 15
PREPARATION TIME: 5–10 MINUTES
CHILLING TIME: 6 HOURS
COOKING TIME: 2–3 MINUTES

130g unsalted butter, softened
1 drop vanilla essence
130g icing sugar

2 large eggs
130g plain flour, sifted

1. Preheat the oven to 220°C/Fan 200°C/Gas 7. Line a baking tray with baking parchment.

2. Beat the butter in a bowl together with the vanilla essence.

3. Add the sugar, and cream until pale in colour.

4. Add the whole eggs, one at a time, beating well until incorporated.

5. Fold in the flour with a metal spoon or spatula.

6. Chill in the fridge for at least 6 hours.

7. Using a spoon, place the biscuit mix on to the prepared baking tray, leaving 5cm between each biscuit to allow for spreading. Press down on each with the back of the spoon.

8. Bake in the preheated oven for 2–3 minutes or until very pale golden brown in colour.

9. Remove from the oven and allow to stand for 1–2 seconds, then remove carefully with a slice or metal spatula.

10. Once made, store in an airtight tin, for up to 1 week.

If possible, chill the mixture in the fridge for as much as 12 hours before use.

To make Palm Tree out of Tuille Biscuits

This is a wonderful dessert recipe – very aesthetically pleasing. It is artistic and was one of the dishes that helped me get my first Michelin star over 16 years ago.

Equipment required   baking tray
1 sharp knife   2 sheets thick plastic
knife sharpener   1 spatula

1. Using a flat piece of plastic (ideally an ice cream container lid), trace out the shape of the top of palm tree and then, using a sharp knife, cut this shape out.

2. Place the plastic lid with its missing palm tree shaped centre on a baking tray. Using a spatula, spread some biscuit mix over this space left behind, making sure there are no gaps.

3. Lift up the lid and there should be a palm tree shaped biscuit on the tray ready for the oven.

4. To make the trunk, cut a rectangle shape out of the middle of plastic lid and, placing on a baking tray, spread with the biscuit mix as with the palm tree top.

5. Cook as page 212.

6. Just before they start to colour, take them out of the oven. Removing carefully with a spatula, place the palm tree top on the base of a round bowl, ladle or coffee cup, pressing gently into the curve. Meanwhile, remove the trunk shape and wrap it tightly round a knife sharpener or similarly shaped kitchen utensil handle, forming a cone shape at one tip. Leave them both to harden.

7. When ready, remove the trunk from the sharpener and place some cream at the cone tip to help it stick. Remove the palm tree from the bowl and place on to the trunk.

8. Serve with the exotic fruit ice parfait on page 59.

Pancakes

This is a very quick and efficient recipe that I used to make when I was a young boy. It saves you a lot of time when you are on a busy market stall or at a fair. It is very versatile – great for savory or sweet recipes.

MAKES: 3–4 PANCAKES
PREPARATION TIME: 5–10 MINUTES
COOKING TIME: 3–4 MINUTES

1 large egg
1 rounded tablespoon plain flour
1–2 tablespoons full-fat milk

pinch salt
pinch sugar
1 teaspoon butter, melted

1. Mix the egg with the flour to a paste.

2. Add the milk very slowly. Use just enough so that you can coat the back of your spoon with the mixture. It should be liquid enough to pour into the pan but if when you run a finger across the back of your spoon, the mixture runs straight down to cover up the mark, it is too thin and you have added too much milk.

3. Stir in a pinch of salt and sugar and the melted butter.

4. Fry them in heavy based pan until golden on each side, roughly 30 seconds.

5. Serve immediately or leave them to cool, each one separated from the other by greaseproof paper.

By melting the butter and adding to the mixture, you save time as you don't then need to add butter to the pan every time you make a pancake.

Aromatic Cream Sauce

This is a very 'cheffy' sauce, but it isn't difficult to prepare, and I guarantee that you will be amazed by its flavour. Whatever you do, make sure when you add the cream and the butter that you don't boil it. It will keep quite easily in a glass bottle. This is a wonderful and creamy veloute sauce that goes well with the royal egg flan trio on page 26, as well as with white meat dishes.

SERVES: 4
PREPARATION TIME: 5 MINUTES
COOKING TIME: 25 MINUTES

1 tablespoon olive oil
70g shallots, peeled and finely chopped
100g button mushrooms, sliced
4 black peppercorns
1 bay leaf
2 whole sprigs fresh thyme
salt and freshly ground black pepper

100ml dry white wine
100ml rich chicken stock
100ml double cream
30g unsalted butter
1 garlic clove, peeled and chopped
4 whole sprigs fresh tarragon

1. Heat the oil in a saucepan and add the shallots, mushrooms, peppercorns, bay leaf, thyme and seasoning. Sweat for 2–3 minutes to soften.

2. Add the white wine, bring to the boil and simmer to reduce by a third, roughly 2–3 minutes.

3. Add the stock, bring back to the boil and simmer to reduce by a third again.

4. Add the double cream, bring back to the boil and immediately remove from the heat.

5. Add the butter, garlic and tarragon, whisk to combine and leave to infuse for 2–3 minutes.

6. Strain through a fine sieve or chinois, pressing down with the back of a ladle. Chill until required. It will keep for 3–4 days in the fridge and will also freeze.

Butter with a Piquant Twist

This is perfect for serving with risottos, pasta or jacket potatoes. It can be frozen in small quantities in ice-cube trays and turned into freezer bags, ready for use.

SERVES: 4–6
PREPARATION TIME: 10 MINUTES
COOKING TIME: 10 MINUTES

20g onions, peeled and finely chopped
10g shallots, peeled and finely chopped
100ml dry white wine

50ml white wine vinegar
200g unsalted butter, cut into pieces

1. Put the onions, shallots, wine and vinegar in a pan and bring to the boil. Continue to simmer for about 5 minutes to reduce by half.

2. Whisk in the butter and remove from the heat to cool slightly.

3. Transfer to a blender or food processor and blitz until smooth. The butter will turn pink.

4. Push through a sieve and then chill until required, or freeze.

Butter Cream Sauce

Unlike the aromatic cream sauce on page 217, which is thin and which it is possible to cook meats in, this recipe is a bit thicker and more powerful – because of the vinegar and the increased amount of butter. You need less of this sauce because of its intensity and it is great as an accompaniment to white fish. For vegetarians and vegetarian dishes, use vegetable stock.

SERVES: 4
PREPARATION TIME: 5 MINUTES
COOKING TIME: 20 MINUTES
INFUSION TIME: 30 MINUTES

knob butter
70g shallots, diced
100g button mushrooms, sliced
4 black peppercorns
1 bay leaf
2 whole sprigs fresh thyme
100ml white wine vinegar

100ml white wine
100ml fish or chicken stock, hot
3–4 tablespoons cream
80–100g unsalted butter
1 garlic clove, halved
4 whole sprigs fresh tarragon

1. In a pan place the knob of butter, shallots, mushrooms, peppercorns, bay leaf and thyme and sweat for 3–4 minutes.

2. Add the vinegar, bring to the boil and simmer to reduce by half, roughly 4 minutes.

3. Add the white wine, bring back to the boil and simmer to reduce by a third again, roughly 6 minutes.

4. Add the hot stock, bring back to the boil and simmer to reduce by a third again, roughly 6 minutes.

5. Add the cream. Heat until almost boiling, then immediately remove from the heat.

6. Add the butter, whisking to combine, and add the garlic and tarragon. Allow to infuse for 30 minutes.

7. Pass through a sieve or strainer, pressing with the back of a ladle to push all of the butter through. Use within 3–4 days.

Proper Tomato Sauce

This sauce not only very useful and extremely tasty but it is also perfect for pasta, for chou farci on page 47, and it goes well with sausages, too! This recipe makes enough for two servings for four people, and will keep in the fridge for a couple of days. It also freezes well. It is guaranteed to be one of the best tomato sauces in the world.

MAKES: 2 PORTIONS FOR 4 PEOPLE
PREPARATION TIME: 10 MINUTES
INFUSION TIME: 30 MINUTES
COOKING TIME: ABOUT 55 MINUTES

2 tablespoons olive oil
100g onions, peeled and finely chopped
100g shallots, peeled and finely chopped
1 whole sprig fresh thyme
2 bay leaves
20ml dry white wine
10g caster sugar

600g chopped canned tomatoes
1 heaped tablespoon tomato purée
20ml extra-virgin olive oil
4 garlic cloves, peeled and halved
bunch fresh basil, leaves whole
To finish
50ml double cream

1. Preheat the oven to 160°C/Fan 140°C/Gas 3.

2. Heat the olive oil in a large ovenproof pan, add the onions, shallots, thyme and bay leaves, and sweat until nicely softened, about 8 minutes.

3. Add the white wine, bring to the boil, then reduce the heat and simmer slowly for about 5 minutes to let it reduce.

4. Add the sugar, and when it has dissolved, add the tomatoes and tomato purée. Lay a sheet of greaseproof paper on top of the tomatoes and bake in the preheated oven for about 40 minutes, or until it has virtually reduced to a paste.

5. Remove from the oven, add the extra-virgin olive oil, garlic and basil, and set the pan on the stove. Heat, stirring, until it comes to the boil.

6. Remove from the heat, cover and leave to infuse for 30 minutes.

7. Remove half of the sauce into a container and set aside to cool (for use in another recipe). Add the cream to the remaining sauce, and warm through gently but do not allow it to boil. Remove the bay leaves. Blend with a hand blender, and serve hot.

For a lighter version, finish it with water instead of cream. For an unusual, richer flavour, add 1/2 vanilla pod instead of the basil at step 5.

Tomato Relish

A tasty homemade relish that is good served with cold and hot meats and fish. It is one of my favourite recipes, which I used to enjoy with my friend Colin Moon (a great British chef) and his wife Hannah.

MAKES: 500ML
PREPARATION TIME: 5 MINUTES
COOKING TIME: 15 MINUTES

1 tablespoon extra-virgin olive oil
1 onion, peeled and finely diced
2 garlic cloves, crushed
1 teaspoon mustard seeds
1 teaspoon coriander seeds
1 red pepper, halved, deseeded and diced

1 red chilli, deseeded and diced
150g caster sugar
salt and freshly ground black pepper
150ml sherry vinegar
1 x 400g can chopped tomatoes
1 teaspoon wholegrain mustard

1. Heat the oil in a heavy-based frying pan.

2. Add the onion, garlic, mustard seeds and coriander seeds, and sweat gently for 1 minute.

3. Add the red pepper and chilli, and cook for a further 2 minutes.

4. Add the sugar, seasoning, vinegar and chopped tomatoes. Cook for 10 minutes over a low heat.

5. Stir in the mustard and remove from the heat.

6. Transfer to a sterilised jar and use within 4–5 days.

Remember to wash your hands after handling the chilli seeds as they are a great irritant if you should touch your eyes.

Monique Basic Dressing

This is a very good basic salad dressing which I use two forks to mix. This will keep for 1 week in the fridge.

MAKES: ABOUT 600ML
PREPARATION TIME: 3 MINUTES

75ml Dijon mustard
50ml red wine vinegar
1 teaspoon caster sugar
2 teaspoons salt
large pinch freshly ground white pepper

100ml warm water
60g shallots, finely diced
1–2 garlic cloves, peeled and finely chopped
300–400ml extra-virgin olive oil

1. Put the mustard, vinegar, sugar, salt, pepper and warm water into a bowl. Stir to combine, and add the shallots and garlic.

2. Pour the oil in gradually, whisking until fully emulsified.

3. Taste on a little bit of salad and adjust the seasoning.

Anchovyade

A speedy anchovy salad dressing that is good to serve tossed into a crisp salad.

MAKES: ROUGHLY 300ML
PREPARATION TIME: 5 MINUTES

1 large egg yolk
75g anchovy fillets in oil, drained
3 garlic cloves, peeled
20 fresh basil leaves
1 tablespoon flat-leaf parsley, chopped

30ml white wine vinegar
30ml Dijon mustard
200ml extra-virgin olive oil
sea salt and freshly ground black pepper
caster sugar, to taste

1. In a food processor or blender, blitz together the egg yolk, anchovies, garlic, herbs, vinegar and mustard.

2. When fully blended, pour the olive oil slowly on to the rotating blades. Season and add sugar to taste. Chill until required.

3. This will keep in the fridge in a clean glass jar for 3–4 days.

To intensify the flavour, add 1 teaspoon tapenade. For a frothy anchovyade, warm the olive oil before adding.

Onion Marmalade

This recipe has a wonderful flavour and keeps well for up to 1 week in the fridge. It would go particularly well with the pâté on page 37.

MAKES: 750ML
PREPARATION TIME: 15 MINUTES
COOKING TIME: 1 HOUR 30 MINUTES

1.5kg red onions
150g butter
750ml red wine

300ml grenadine
lemon juice

1. Slice the onions thinly, taking the root out and cutting across the grain.

2. Melt the butter in a heavy-based pan. When melted, add the onions and cook for 1 minute.

3. Add the wine and bring to the boil. Continue to simmer until reduced, roughly 20 minutes.

4. Add the grenadine and continue to cook for 10–15 minutes.

5. When it has achieved the consistency of marmalade, add a dash of lemon juice.

6. Take off the heat and place in sterilised jars. Use within 4–5 days.

Rémoulade

A very quick and tasty celeriac salad, this makes a pleasant change from green salads.

MAKES: 8 PORTIONS
PREPARATION TIME: 5 MINUTES

1 small head celeriac
1 tablespoon lemon juice
1 teaspoon wholegrain mustard

1 teaspoon horseradish
3 tablespoons mayonnaise
salt and freshly ground black pepper

1. Peel the celeriac and cut immediately into fine julienne strips. As soon as the strips are cut, stir into the lemon juice to prevent discoloration.

2. In a separate bowl, mix together the mustard, horseradish and mayonnaise, and season. Stir in the celeriac.

3. Cover and chill. Use within 2–3 days.

The celeriac should only be prepared at the last possible moment as it discolours very quickly once cut.

Piccalilli

A homemade pickle that is great served with cheese or cold cooked meats.

MAKES: 500 ML
PREPARATION TIME: 25 MINUTES
COOKING TIME: 40–50 MINUTES

¼ head of cauliflower
½ cucumber
½ red pepper, deseeded
½ stick of celery
250g silverskin onions, peeled
50ml extra-virgin olive oil
salt and freshly ground black pepper
15g mustard seeds, toasted

15g fennel seeds
10g ground turmeric
½ teaspoon English mustard powder
1 level teaspoon cornflour
12g caster sugar
40g fresh root ginger, finely diced
250ml white wine vinegar

1. Trim the cauliflower into 3mm florets. Plunge into a pan of salted boiling water and blanch for about 3 minutes. Drain and plunge into iced water. When cooled, drain well.

2. Cut the cucumber, red pepper, celery and onions into 3mm pieces.

3. In a large pan, heat the olive oil. Add the onions, celery and red pepper. Season, stir and cook at a medium heat for 3 minutes.

4. Add the cauliflower and cucumber, and cook for a further 3 minutes.

5. Add the seeds, turmeric, mustard powder, cornflour, sugar and ginger, and cook for a further 5 minutes.

6. Add the vinegar, reduce the heat and cook gently for 20 minutes, or until the vegetables are cooked but still crisp.

7. Check the consistency. If it is too thick, add a little water.

8. Remove from the heat, allow to cool a little, then ladle into hot sterilised glass preserving jars. Label and store in a cool dry place for up to a week.

Fresh Herb Oil

I make this with herbs from my organic 'edible garden' when we run the Summer Academy. Use this method with any type or combination of very soft green herb. It is a delicious dressing and can be frozen in small quantities.

MAKES: 800ML
PREPARATION TIME: 15 MINUTES, PLUS 1 HOUR DRAINING TIME

1 garlic clove, peeled
200ml water
50g fresh tarragon
50g fresh mint
50g fresh basil leaves

50g fresh flat-leaf parsley
50g fresh coriander
100g watercress
salt, to taste
250ml olive oil

1. In a food processor or blender, blitz the garlic, water, herbs, watercress and salt until blended.

2. Pass through a conical strainer suspended over a large pan, pressing with the back of a ladle to remove all the liquid. Reserve the liquid in the pan but discard the roughage left behind. Wash out the sieve or strainer and line with muslin.

3. Bring the liquid almost to boiling point, then remove from the heat and pour through the muslin-lined sieve or strainer. Leave to drain for 1 hour.

4. Discard the liquid but reserve the residue left on the muslin. Turn into a large bowl, add the olive oil and whisk to combine until emulsified.

5. Pour into a glass bottle and store in the fridge.

Walnut Dip

This recipe makes a nice change from the ordinary spreads and dips in supermarkets, plus it contains no additives.

SERVES: 2–4
PREPARATION TIME: 5 MINUTES
CHILLING TIME: 30 MINUTES

3 tablespoons crème fraîche
1 tablespoon shelled walnuts, finely chopped

2 garlic cloves, peeled and finely sliced
juice of ½ small lemon
20g fresh chervil, chopped

1. Combine all the ingredients.

2. Chill for 30 minutes before serving.

Stock Syrup

This is a basic stock syrup for making ice-creams, sorbets etc. You will need a chef's thermometer.

MAKES: 300ML
PREPARATION TIME: 2–3 MINUTES
COOKING TIME: 20 MINUTES

200g granulated sugar
100ml cold water

1. Put the sugar and water into a heavy-based pan over a low heat and stir until the sugar is dissolved.

2. Slowly bring to the boil and continue to boil until it reaches 102–104°C, but make sure the stock does not brown or caramelise.

3. When it is ready, bubbles will begin to appear and the stock looks syrupy. Remove from the heat and allow to cool.

4. When cool, store in a glass jar in the fridge or freeze. Use within 1 week.

Make sure that the sugar is fully dissolved before bringing it to the boil, otherwise the stock will crystallise. A safe way to avoid sugar crystallisation is to use sugar cubes, which contain fewer impurities but cook in the same way as loose sugar. To flavour the syrup with alcohol, add 2 parts syrup to 1 part of your chosen spirit and pour into the warmed stock syrup at step 3, after removing from the heat.

Crème Pâtissière

This is a French classic and a foolproof recipe for filling cakes, pastries etc.

MAKES: 700G
PREPARATION TIME: 10 MINUTES
COOKING TIME: 5–8 MINUTES

50g plain flour, sifted
4 medium egg yolks
30g custard powder

500ml milk
175g caster sugar
1 vanilla pod, halved lengthways

1. Tip the flour, eggs and custard powder into a bowl and combine well together to form a thin batter.

2. Pour the milk into a heavy-based pan with the sugar and vanilla pod and bring to the boil, stirring to dissolve the sugar. Remove immediately from the heat and pour in the batter, stirring constantly, until a paste is formed.

3. Pour back into the pan and bring back to the boil. Turn down the heat immediately to low and cook, stirring continuously with a wooden spoon, until thickened. Remove the vanilla pod. (It is important to turn down the heat quickly to prevent the custard from catching on the bottom of the pan.)

4. Pour into a container and allow to cool, covered with cling film to prevent a skin from forming. Chill before use.

For a light crème pâtissière, add 30ml kirsch and 75ml whipping cream to 200ml of the basic recipe .

Coconut Cream

This is great in the Eton mess on page 72 or as an alternative to the crème fraîche served with the tartes fines on page 61.

SERVES: 4
PREPARATION TIME: 2 MINUTES

100ml coconut milk
50ml crème fraîche
1 teaspoon caster sugar

1. Whisk together the milk and the crème fraîche. When combined, fold in the sugar.

2. Cover and chill until required. Use within 4–5 days.

Make sure you keep it chilled at all times.

Iced White Chocolate with Whisky

Probably the most sensual recipe of the book, it is best eaten in the evening while watching depressing TV.

SERVES: 6–12
PREPARATION TIME: 5 MINUTES
FREEZER TIME: 1 HOUR

200g white chocolate
20ml whisky, chilled
180ml double cream, chilled

1. Break the chocolate into very small pieces. Put a non-stick saucepan on a low heat until just warm. Remove from the heat.

2. Add the white chocolate and stir with a wooden spoon so that the chocolate melts very slowly.

3. Add the whisky and double cream straight from the fridge. Continue stirring until slight ribbons form.

4. Pour into an ice-cube tray or ice-lolly moulds and freeze for at least 1 hour.

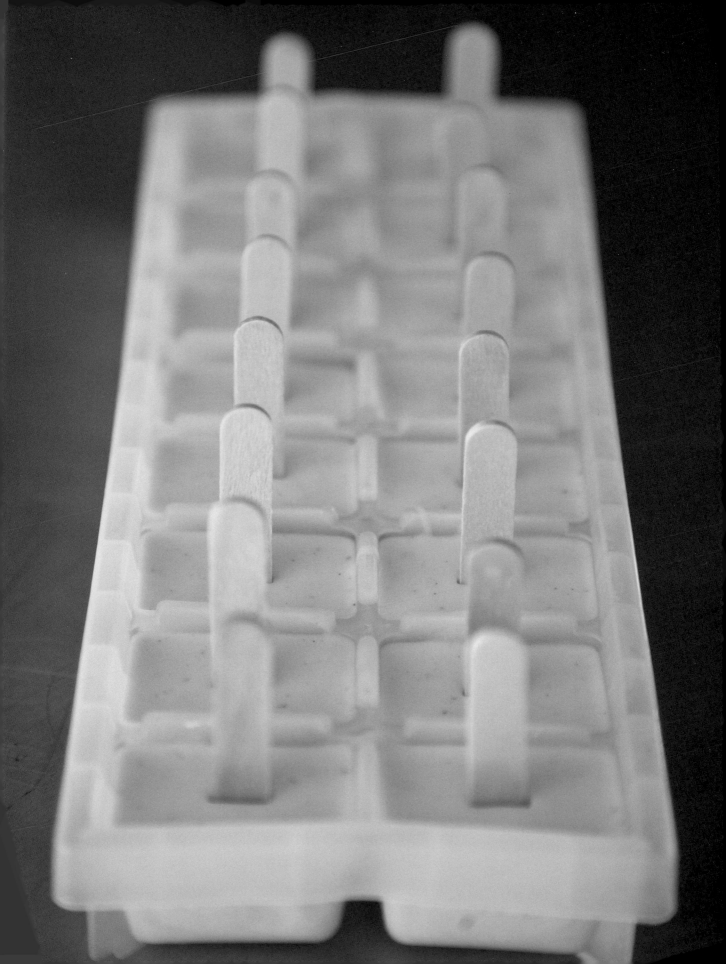

index

almonds
    chocolate macaroon yo-yos 90–1
    poached salmon, leek and blue cheese quiche
      16–17
    rocher 87–9
    white chocolate and passion fruit toffee cup 120
anchovies
    anchovy, goat's cheese and orange salad 42
    anchovyade 223–5
    sweet gazpacho with herby crab mayonnaise 36
apples
    baked apple soufflés with chocolate and kirsch
      sauce 152–3
    baked glazed apples 68–71
    wake-up smoothie 2
apricots: hot apricot flan 119
asparagus: baked aubergines with baby vegetables
    108–9
aubergines
    aubergine hummus 178–9
    baked aubergines with baby vegetables 108–9
    home-fed mussels with vanilla piperade 102–3
    spiced aubergine wrapped in Parma ham 23–5
avocados: tuna steak tartare rapido 48

bacon
    Crouchmoor Farm breakfast 28–33
    Flemish tart 12
    home-fed mussels with vanilla piperade 102–3
    see also pancetta
bananas
    caramelised banana splits with rum and
      chocolate sauce 84–5
    wake-up smoothie 2
beef
    best beef and cheese lasagne 112–13
    childhood baked stuffed tomatoes 177
    minute steak with tomato relish 181
    oven-glazed beef fillet 'Mich Mich' 144–5
beetroot: chilled beetroot gazpacho 129
biscuits
    chocolate macaroon yo-yos 90–1
    Fox's Mint bonbon tuile biscuit 86
    tuille biscuits 212–15
black pudding
    baby squid, chorizo, black pudding, anchovy
      and poached egg salad 38–41
    Crouchmoor Farm breakfast 28–33
blackcurrants: spiced mixed beries with yogurt
    4–7
blueberries: spiced mixed beries with yogurt 4–7
bread
    anchovy, goat's cheese and orange salad 42
    brioche 18–21
    Camembert bread 170–1
    croque madame 22
    minute steak with tomato relish 181

    my own French onion soup 166–9
    pain de mie 201
    tuna steak tartare rapido 48
brioche 18–21
broad beans: Monique Nibolitta broth with smoked
    aioli 98–9
butter
butter cream sauce 219
butter with a piquant twist 218
butternut squash: roast chicken crown with sweet
    lemon and thyme 142–3

cabbage
    chou farci 46–7
    pommes boulangère maman Novelli 190
cannellini beans: Monique Nibolitta broth with
    smoked aioli 98–9
capers
    crispy ham and cheese pork chop cappuccio
      186–7
    salmon en croûte 104–7
    tuna steak tartare rapido 48
carrots
    bamboo-steamed monkfish osso-bucco style
      136–7
    lentil fricassee 196–7
    Merlot-braised oxtail with pan-fried ricotta
      gnocchi 110–11
    Monique Nibolitta broth with smoked aioli 98–9
    vegetable nage 200
cauliflower: piccalilli 229–31
celeriac: rémoulade 228
celery
    lentil fricassee 196–7
    Monique Nibolitta broth with smoked aioli 98–9
    piccalilli 229–31
    poached salmon, leek and blue cheese quiche
      16–17
    sweet curried seafood stew with beer 52–3
    vegetable nage 200
cheese
    baked aubergines with baby vegetables 108–9
    baked cod dauphinois 140–1
    baked Vacherin cheese with Iberico ham 173–5
    best beef and cheese lasagne 112–13
    Camembert bread 170–1
    childhood baked stuffed tomatoes 177
    cod brandade glazed with red peppers 100–1
    crispy ham and cheese pork chop cappuccio
      186–7
    croque madame 22
    Crouchmoor Farm breakfast 28–33
    gratin dauphinois à la Jean de Vienne 191
    ham and cheese beignets 66
    Merlot-braised oxtail with pan-fried ricotta
      gnocchi 110–11
    minute steak with tomato relish 181

EVERYDAY NOVELLI

INDEX